Jim Douglas

CW00859855

TEENAGE

TO

TRAVELITIS

"Growing up in q World of Jazz"

Jim Douglas

Jim Douglas

Jim Douglas

ISBN-10: 1519573774
ISBN-13: 9781519573773

ACKNOWLEDGMENTS

I would like to thank each and every one of you, dear readers, who so graciously bought my first published effort: *"Tunes, Tours and Travelitis".* To have actually read it and even find time to award me with twenty five-star ratings is a miracle in itself to me. I experienced a great deal of fun and nostalgia in writing it and it seems you did too!

"Teenage to Travelitis" is not so much a sequel as a prequel inasmuch as it covers the years from my teens and includes untold revelations in the duo decade before my fortieth birthday. I would like to also thank Pete Kerr for his friendship and inspiration in our teenage years, his involvement in recording Alex's band in the 1960s and his help in publishing both books.

Lastly, I owe an everlasting debt of gratitude to my wife Maggie and son Will, without whose love, patience, understanding and help this effort would never have seen the light of day My sincere thanks to all of you for enabling me to chronicle what so far has been an extraordinary existence.
Jim Douglas

Jim Douglas

DEDICATION

To all my friends and colleagues who have supported and
inspired me for the last half century in my life in jazz

Jim Douglas

CONTENTS

Introduction

Foreword

PART ONE "Teenage"

Jim Douglas

PART TWO: "Travelitis"

PART THREE: "Retirement"

Foreword

By Will Douglas

Hey, how are you doing? I hope you've been well since the last book.

Wasn't it fun? Not bad for twenty years' work. Fortunately for you and, indeed, me, my dad caught the bug and wrote the pre-sequel in one-tenth the time, whilst being twenty(ish) years older than he was when he started the first. That alone should stand as a testament to the importance of the memories herein.

Anyway.

When I first half-drunkenly offered to write a foreword for my father's second book, I suppose

I assumed at the time that I'd just gush uncontrollably about how much I love and respect him, of course.

But, actually, then I thought, as I tend to from time to time, about the possibility, nay potential, of my saying something worthwhile with this space, and thus was the following born.

I like telling and hearing stories; I think storytelling is key to the human experience. In fact, I think that the first thing we probably did after inventing language was start telling each other about what we'd done, where we'd been and the things we'd seen as a way of sharing ourselves with those who couldn't have been there. One of the greatest benefits of being human, as opposed to a different animal, is to be able to share your memories and experiences with each other and create a tapestry of ideas and shared memories together. And so I've always got time to listen to somebody's story, and heaven (or Valhalla or nirvana, pick your poison) knows that I've heard a few dozen of the best during my tenure as the offspring of the author, many of which I'm sure you are already familiar with (unless you didn't read the first book, in which case, I'd recommend that you find and ingest it as soon as physically possible).

I honestly can't tell you how many times I've heard some of these stories, though I suspect some may total in the near-hundreds. I've heard them so much I could probably regurgitate them verbatim, and I've certainly regaled my own friends with The Legend of Bix Duff or The Tale of Lenny Hastings and the Church Bells. You, like me, I assume, are probably a fan of these characters (maybe you even got to meet some of them!) and I expect you will have enormous amounts of fun reimagining them over the coming pages. I've felt like I've known many of these immortals for my entire life, despite many of them having sadly passed before I was even the proverbial twinkle in Mr. Douglas senior's eye.

To illustrate this point, I want you to

imagine that you are a child of – let's say – nine years old, sitting at a table with your parents and half a dozen or so of their friends, also band members, also swapping stories. The laughter is raucous and as you watch them spilling their drinks and slapping the table with laughter, you don't quite understand why it's funny but you might, just, possibly, have found some of the greatest people you are ever likely to meet. Every story is told with deference, every insulting impression homage. It isn't hard to wish you were there, to have known in the moment of the punchline that you had new fodder for the next bar room table at which you would hold forum.

Because it was always bar room tables. Of course it was. (Hell, I stealthily planned what I'd say in this blurb whilst in the pub with the old man only an hour before the time of writing!) And if the walls in the Dog & Sausage, St. Helier, Jersey could talk….

These are jazz musicians, of course, and, as I learned at a very young age, there are three things that go into being a renowned 'jazzer':

1. Drinking.

2. Telling hilarious stories about each other.

3. Possibly possessing some aptitude with a musical instrument.

- definitely in that order. And to be the musician's musician, you'd better be damned good at getting the accent right!

My father is someone I would call the musician's musician, as I honestly don't know any who don't hold his talent and character in the highest esteem (though statistically they must be out there somewhere).

So then, when on a recent excursion to Croatia as part of a band of these sorts of legends, I was asked to participate in a Q&A session with the band, I anticipated very quickly the only question anyone would want to ask me;

the same question everyone always asks me.

"What is it like being Jim Douglas' son?"

So, in an effort to pre-empt any further inquisition, here is my reply.

Being Jim's son is as hard as trying to follow his solo in a band, but when you're done playing whatever-the-hell it was you played, you look up and he's smiling at you with encouraging pride. As are all his friends, many of whom feature in the pages following this foreword. I hope you'll enjoy this second trip down memory lane from a man who has been lucky enough to do what he loves for most of his life and still loves it as much now as he did then.

It ain't easy being the sequel, so I hope you'll be as kind to this book as the guest stars within have been to me.

INTRODUCTION

I can't eat raw tomatoes, cucumber or, on some occasions, onions. Cooked? Fine! The reason is lodged somewhere in my distant memory. My maternal grandfather is to blame. There was nothing he liked better. Lovingly perching me on his tweed-clad knee, which smelled of sheep and pipe tobacco, he would feed me tit-bits which I adoringly forced down. I was about two years old.

I was born at the seventh month of my mother's first pregnancy, entering the world with no fingernails and congested lungs. My mother had contracted mumps. Rather than wait for any other damage, I had decided on an early stage appearance. My audience, consisting of my parents and grandparents and wise old stage hand, midwife Nurse MacBain, welcomed me with trepidation and bewilderment at my size. I weighed seven and a half pounds at thirty-four weeks which makes me wonder what I could have been if I had gone full term.

My grandfather, James Elliot, was a shepherd on the estate of Newton Hall, owned by a retired army officer, one Captain Butter by name, who had discovered the dubious joys of hunting big game. My grandmother Beatrice and mother, Agnes (Nancy) were in his service. When war broke out in 1939, his mansion house, which had some lineage to Sir Isaac Newton, was inhabited by the Royal Army Medical Corps in which my father, Private Kenneth Douglas practised bandaging and hanging arms in slings between executing two-stroke rolls, flams and drags in their Pipe band drum section. With his "Brylcreemed" hair, fashionable 'nerdy' spectacles and his over-large horsehair sporran he was a sight to behold! Or in my mother's case, someone to fall in love with. I do hope they were in love! They were at least attracted to each other enough because, sometime in the late summer months of 1941, I was conceived.

That same year, my father had embarked on the hellish journey to Dunkirk, after the 'little boats' had performed their heroic miracle, in the clean-up operations. I think it was on his return that my conception, perhaps less than immaculate, was attained. During the next few months, probably as a direct result of what he had experienced, his nervous system deteriorated and, after compassionate leave to marry my expectant mother, he was discharged from the Army. I have a feeling that, being a city-born man, he was a bit like a fish out of water in the pastoral environment of a shepherd and his flock.

Things were about to change, however. The war ended and things were slowly returning to some sort of normality when disaster struck. My grandfather, who had been recognised as an excellent breeder and trainer of Border Collies, had gone one step farther in being asked to officiate as a judge at sheep dog trials. It was while performing this task at one such meeting that he suddenly collapsed and died from a heart attack. He was forty –nine years old. Out of grief and shock, my mother, who was by this time, pregnant with my brother Ian, was delivered of a second premature baby in the eighth month of her gestation. With the main breadwinner gone, the tied house that went with his position had to be vacated for the arrival of a successor. My grandmother gathered her flock about her, acquired a council-owned, three-bedroomed, semi-detached bungalow in the beautiful, historic village of Gifford, in the Parish of Yester, three miles from Newton Hall and took vacant possession. She took the front bedroom, her nine-year-old son, my uncle Jake, moved into the middle, box room, leaving the largest room at the rear of the house to her daughter, husband and young family. At first, while she gradually overcame her grief, the family united in their quest to face the post-war future.

At this point I should tell you of a hereditary eye disease that affected her. Her maiden name was Brodie. Her brother John, son Jake, and she were the last in the line to carry this affliction, which manifested itself in a drying and cracking of the cornea, causing pain and partial sight loss. To make matters worse, she had ventured outside one evening and in the blackness and unfamiliarity of her new environment, had walked into an unseen, face-level washing line and scarred the better of her two affected eyes. From that time on, she virtually became housebound, relying on my mother to take care of extra-domestic chores such as shopping and the like.

Looking back and reading between the lines, I now realise that my father had little in common with either her or her way of life. I believe she had already 'found' a husband for her daughter in the shape of a local fellow shepherd with whom my mother had been slightly more than 'on speaking terms'. My father's arrival threw a hefty spanner into those works. I think she took over, as reliable mothers-in-law do. My dad had been brought up under much more disciplinary rules than she extended to her family

Through financial circumstances caused by the premature death of his own, my father had been required to leave school at fourteen to enable his older brother to graduate through university as an architect.   By no means an academic slouch himself, I think he felt resentment as a result. The situation now, sadly, caused more. His parental duties as he saw them were being over-ridden, leaving him with a decision to make: to put up with it or to move his young family away. Choosing the latter, In the early months of 1947 he found employment as a timekeeper/clerk with the Scottish Motor Traction, a company responsible for public transport in Edinburgh.   After successfully applying for and getting a 'prefab' in a developing area on the outskirts of the city at Sighthill, he moved back to the place of his roots.

Over the next decade the family

underwent many changes. Not earning sufficient wages to support his young family, which had grown after the birth of a third son, Dick, my father had decided to move back to Gifford. This, of course, meant living with my grandmother again while he looked for work. But he and my granny just didn't see things the same way. Row after row ensued with my mother always coming down on her mother's side. He found employment as a timekeeper/clerk for a local builder who had a contract to erect a reservoir at a tiny hamlet called Longformacus. My sister, Sheena, had recently been born and I think this period was the happiest in the family's time together. On completion of the contract, back we went to granny! The conflict started again so he decided to apply for a council house. We were granted a three-bedroomed, pre-assembled, semi-detached house just around the corner from granny's bungalow and four doors away from my mother's brother, Wattie, and his similar-sized family.

From then until the time I left for

Germany and London in 1960, which you will read about in due course, if you decide to carry on after my ramblings here, I enjoyed a wonderful life.

Granny moved in with us because of her developing blindness which meant my father was finding live-in jobs all around the country, only returning once a month or so to see his growing family. There were now five of us after the birth of my youngest brother, Alan. My education went upwards in leaps and bounds, resulting in my achieving the coveted 'Dux of the School' award and a place in the top class at my new school, the 'Knox Academy' which was named after the Presbyterian, religious reformer of the same name, who had been born and raised in the area.

There were more good times than bad: sledging in the snow-covered fields in the winter, disappearing for hours on end to explore woods and hillsides in the summer, fancy-dress school concerts in the village hall, dressing up for 'guising' at "Hallowe'en', Christmas celebrations, rolling Easter eggs, adolescent crushes, eavesdropping on 'first footers' from the top of the stairs at 'Hogmanay' and listening to the 'Goon Show' on our old wireless. It was endless!

My parents and a lot of my friends have gone now, either from existence itself or from my personal memory. What follows is as near an accurate recollection of my life in jazz and the rewards the music brought me as I can remember. There are still a few folks around on whom I can rely to correct me when my mind plays tricks.   It has been fun recalling my adventures but not as much fun as I had when they were happening.   I have had a wonderful life; I hope you agree!

Jim Douglas

Bridesmaid, Jennie Fairgrieve; My Father; Mother and Uncle, Alan

PART ONE

"Teenage"

Chapter One

"The Italian Job"

At fifteen years of age, my life was a conundrum of quadrilateral equations, Latin verbs, thoughts of the opposite sex and *flams* and *paradiddles.* To elucidate, I was trying to concentrate on a Scottish Higher education while, simultaneously, being sexually awakened by the sight of among others, the beautiful Christine Milne, with whom I was besotted, and learning to play pipe band drumming in the Boys'

Brigade. I succeeded in the first category, failed miserably in the second and reached the heights of mediocrity in the latter. By thrashing about on a very nice Premier side-drum, I slowly achieved a technical standard that stopped my parents shouting for me to "shut that din up, for God's sake" and allowed me to seriously consider joining a band with school mate, bagpiper Pete Kerr.

My school career was, for the most part, following a pretty steady rise up the graph to educational acceptance. I had left both my primary schools with glowing results, having achieved a mock 'pass' in the 'qualifying examinations' which determined your grade in Secondary school, when I was only seven years old. (There were only fourteen pupils in the entire school at the Lammermoor hamlet of Longformacus, where my father had found employment and I had been given the chance to 'run with the pack', and later gained a bona fide result when I was the proper age of around twelve. I have been told since that my pass mark was one of the highest ever in East Lothian, but I had had plenty of practice and actually enjoyed studying. School swot – that was me!

I was given an "A" grade which meant being accepted into the 'top tier' for my first term at Knox Academy Secondary school, named after the famous Presbyterian reformer and which was situated in the County town of Haddington, four miles or so from the village of Gifford where I lived. After one-on-one teaching, the system of having hour-long periods covering different subject matters, with different teachers in different rooms, threw me off my tracks for a while, as did meeting and working with new 'friends', but I eventually settled into the system. I must say, though, that I don't think I had or, for that matter, have, ever come across a more varied bunch of eccentrics as the teachers I had now come face to face with.

My form-teacher was Miss Burnett who taught English and French. An ample-bosomed lady in the latter years of her third decade, perhaps, she would swish into the class room, subconsciously closing the lapels of her gown over her breasts, while simultaneously giving them a sly massage – an action which could never go unnoticed by a dozen spotty-faced adolescent young men and an equal number of self -conscious girls in the process of growing some of their own!

"Bonjour mes amis!"

was her greeting.

"Bonjour Madame!"

was our reply, while to a man (and woman) getting to our feet and massaging our own breasts, imaginary or otherwise. She never noticed our parodic response, having already turned around to sit down at her table.

Then there was Mr. Sutherland who, for some unknown reason lost in the passage of time, became known as 'Zoran'. He was our Maths teacher and could be Insufferable in morning classes, but passably tolerant in the afternoon after a couple of lunchtime whiskies in the local pub. His little reward for inattention or even just failing to grasp his grumpy instructions, was a flick with a wooden ruler behind the ear or, when held sideways between his fingers, a painful wrap on the knuckles. We endured 'Wavy' Davey, our stink-bomb aficionado Science Master, who seemed to like nothing better than to have the class produce sulphur-based, 'fart-like' smells which filled an already permeated classroom. We loved 'Granny' Weir, our forever smiling Art Mistress, who had beautiful freckled skin and the first gold fillings I had ever seen, in her teeth. She wore her long, slightly greying hair, in a 'bun' which probably earned her nickname.

Probably the most fascinating of them all was Robert 'Wee Bill' Wilson, our Latin enthusiast and Classics master. Small in stature, with an old fashioned approach to life (he would always touch his hat to you if you passed in the street), he nursed a gigantic, sometimes uncontrollable, temper. He demanded total concentration in his classes which, I suppose, was all he felt he deserved. His accoutrements included a small brown 'Globetrotter' suitcase, which was placed on his desk next to his hat. If any miscreant dared to let his attention waver from his lessons, or his or her homework was not up to his demanding expectations, this 'projectile' would suddenly be hurled through the air to land uncannily accurately on the desk of the perpetrator in question:

"Open that suitcase and bring its content to me!"

came the bellowed instruction from the teacher, red-faced and blinking furiously with one slightly dodgy-looking eye. On opening the case, the recipient would find a long, thick, two-tongued strap of leather in it. This was the notorious Scottish 'Tawse', a mediaeval, torturous implement, thankfully now banned from use. The guilty pupil, crestfallen with the anticipation of what he or she (there was no gender differential) knew was to come, would then walk slowly to the front of the class, return the 'belt' to its owner, stretch out one upturned hand and wait for the descent of the painful, atrocious punishment the master would dole out. Depending on the situation, the gravity of the offence or perhaps even the mood of the punisher, this could be of anything up to six strokes, the maximum legally allowed, I believe. Sometimes even, depending on the flagellator's degree of 'sadism', one hand would be positioned under the other resulting in a double whammy!

Our music teacher, who was also the local Scout Master, was George 'Schnozzle' Robertson. He introduced me to choir singing and the 'Classics', bringing a new meaning to the names Beethoven, Bach, Handel and Mozart – merely vaguely stored in my musically undeveloped brain. To interest us in Prokofiev's 'Peter and the Wolf', which was to resurrect itself to me at a later date, played in a different style, he produced a costumed concert performance. The picture above displays the cast. I don't remember any drum solos in the original manuscript. but the school audience got plenty from a budding, painted-moustachioed, tin soldier percussionist on this occasion. You can't keep a good adolescent down!

But enough of school and its halcyon days, as someone once described them and on with the real subject in hand!

There was unabashed heroism on my part for eighteen-month older Peter Kerr, prefect and head boy. He was in the sixth form at school, studying art, a path down which I fully intended to follow, in my desire to emulate my uncle Alan Douglas by having the letters ARIBA after my name. Pete has proved to be one of nature's talents in the way he has succeeded in most of the career directions he has followed during his still busy lifetime, whether in music, art or lately, writing best-selling books. But the new "Skiffle" craze had other plans for me with the sound of Lonnie Donegan, Chas McDevitt and

"The Vipers", playing constantly in my mind. My Uncle Jake, who being only seven years my senior, and thus was more like a brother, had arrived home from National Service in Egypt with an un-restorable, un-playable guitar with which I fell totally in love and which sowed dreams of my playing in a band such as those of my heroes. In moments of private, pretend practice which included imaginary performances to enthralled audiences, I strummed this adored stringless instrument. Could this be the first instance of "air guitar" perhaps?

I desperately, totally unreasonably, pleaded with my poor mother to buy me a playable guitar for my forthcoming birthday, knowing full well it was way beyond her means. In the meantime, I had arranged to undertake a bicycle trip around Scotland with two fellow school mates at the beginning of the summer break, planning to stop overnight at Youth Hostels at the end of each daily journey. This was a wonderful experience during which I discovered date, cheese and jam and various other exotically-filled sandwiches and bottled beer, bought without question of age from a licensed grocer in Tomintoul, one of the highest villages in Scotland, where we had arrived completely knackered from the ascent we had climbed to reach it. Our ensuing ale-affected descent was a joyous cacophony of shouts, whoops and songs, delivered at record-breaking speed for a bicycle. An early instance of "Travelitis"?

We had a wonderful holiday taking in the splendours of Perth, Aberdeen, Inverness, Loch Ness, Fort William, Glen Coe and the 'Trossachs' before returning to Edinburgh around about midnight on the last stage, completely spent. I remember being unable to face the last nineteen miles back to my home in the beautiful village of Gifford and climbing into a laundry hamper in Waverley Station to spend the night. All thoughts of guitars and 'Skiffle' had almost faded in the exhilaration of the trip. Waking up cold but refreshed at dawn, I set off homewards. On reaching the little gate of my home I was greeted by an obviously anxious but relieved mother, my grandmother and four curious, excited siblings.

"Welcome hame son and a happy belated birthday tae ye, there's a wee present for ye in the lobby!"

My mother's words, both, at the same time, caring and arousing curiosity, were joyous to hear. Weary, but excited by the whole occasion, I opened the door into the "lobby". I couldn't believe what met my eyes! There, leaning against the front door was a trapezium shaped cardboard box which could only contain one thing – a guitar! I tore open the package and there it was, and I still have it, a guitar sent by mail order all the way from Italy. I didn't know whether to shout, laugh or cry and probably did all three!

Jim Douglas

"You'd better learn tae play it, noo!"

said my granny.

"Ah will and Ah'll start richt away!"

I replied and sitting down on the sofa, I cuddled the already beloved instrument in my arms and promptly fell into a deep dream-filled sleep.

And so the adventure that was to lead me to interesting cities, towns and villages with their halls, hotels and pubs, where I would meet and form new friendships, discover new ways of playing my music with new colleagues and, at a later stage, my heroes from my first aspirations and inspirations, began.

Like most things in life worth learning, the process doesn't come easy. The guitar is no exception! From the initial tuning 'trial' to discovering where to place one's fingers on the frets to encourage a clear note, to finding the correct clamp-like pressure to form a chord in which all the notes sound undistorted and even, is a frustration in itself. Then you have to learn to change and move chords in time to the music, not to mention scales, arpeggios and other necessary requirements to become anything other than 'just another guitar owner'. In my case, two people came to my rescue: The former was, unknown to him, guitarist Bert Weedon, who had published a simple beginner's guitar tutorial called "Play in a Day" which I purchased out of my earnings from my Saturday job at the local butcher's shop. I opened the glossy volume in excitement and anticipation. True to his promise, with a bit of determination and rapidly tiring, aching fingers, I was able to strum a simple song with which, in a breaking Scottish voice I "beguiled" my "amazed" family. I was up and running! No stopping me now! This was going to be a piece of cake!! (In later years I was to meet Bert Weedon who, as 'Chief Water-rat' was presiding over a function I had been booked to play at in London's famous Grosvenor House. He was most interested in my career, nurtured by his original inspiration and a charming, nice chap he was, indeed!)

My second benefactor was none other than my uncle, who lived three doors away. Walter, or Wattie, as we knew him, had at some stage in his National Service, plucked a double bass, so therefore became my source of criticism and encouragement. He gave me both in different degrees. The first

"Aye, no too bad son!"

was often followed by a

"If ye keep it up ye'll get it richt afore lang!"

Disappointed but, at the same time, heartened I returned home to practise a bit more. Wattie was probably the best person I could ever have known at the start of a musical career. When I did get it right there was no one more delighted and encouraging. I owe a great deal of gratitude to his memory. Daily I would get up early to practise a bit before getting ready for school, rush home for a bit more before doing my homework and hurriedly eating my tea, then rush up to Wattie's house for my latest assessment! The first thing I played with any conviction was the old Blues number, "It takes a Worried Man to Sing a Worried Song". complete with a one finger on one string introduction and sung in a squeaky Scottish voice. The next step was obvious - I needed a Skiffle Group! The easiest way was to form my own with my brothers, Ian on washboard, Dick on oil drum and broom handle bass and my sister, Sheena on spoons. Occasionally my mother joined in on Jew's harp and my granny, complete with glass of elderberry wine and essential cigarette, would peer at us through partially sighted eyes and emit such encouragements as

"Gaun yersel', Son!"

Word reached me of a lad called Graham Cassie, a banker's son, who lived in the nearby market town of Haddington and who had also been learning the guitar with a view to forming a group and, although my memory has let me down regarding how it came about, I joined forces with him and another guitar player called Alec Young, a washboard enthusiast, Derek Dewar, a printer from the staff of the local newspaper, John Logan on tea chest bass and a nice singer, Nita Cowley. (She is still singing and has a successful career as Benita Baugh.) We called the group "The Tynesiders" with reference to the river which served the industry in the town at the time and shares its name with its bigger sister in Newcastle upon Tyne.

After hours of practice, listening to records, and collating a very minimal list of songs, we were invited to play at the local British Legion Club - a half-hour spot or so, exhausting our repertoire, followed by our dubious accompaniment of guests and member, "singers." Most of their names have long disappeared in the mists of time, although their faces pop up in weird pockets of photographically-induced memory. One chap though, suspiciously known as "Fishy" McAlpine, is irremovably stuck in my fond reminiscences. He stood well over six foot in his stockinged feet and was as lean as he was long. With his pale, sallow complexion crowned by a well brilliantine-anointed, neatly-barbered mat of jet black hair combed straight back in the Bela Lugosi "Dracula" style, his Celtic blue eyes peered out in slightly different directions and a droopy, soggy roll-up dangled from his lips. His well-presented attire consisting of highly polished toe-capped shoes, knife-edge-pressed charcoal-grey trousers, white-collared shirt and black tie, the whole ensemble was finished by the accoutrement of a black, mohair and wool, "Crombie" style overcoat. His choice of song was just as funereal! Standing almost to attention at the microphone, he would open his mouth just enough to enable him to restrain the rancid roll-up and emit a high- pitched whine. With a sob in his throat he offered two 'beauties': "Take a Message to my Mother!" and "Just a Little Bit of Khaki that my Father Wore at Mons!" Wonderful! They don't write or make them like that anymore. As a sixteen-year-old I'd had an occasional, sneaky under-age drink with my Dad in the local pub but the British Legion Club gave me my drinking "A" Levels! Shouts like:

"Gie the wee yin a pint!"

and:

"Aye, he deserves yin!"

together with some beverages even delivered to the stage by hand, it was ensured I never left the place less than "stotious!" There was no way I could get home, even if I had wanted to and I accepted Alec Young's magnanimous offer of his 'put-u-up' with gratitude and anticipation of a Sunday spent with him and his attractive new wife, Janet, the "News of the World" and a lunch which always ended with home-made mandarin flan, topped with Nestlé's sterilized whipped cream. (Yum, yum!) We would hone our guitar skills or lack thereof, share our dreams and hopes for the future and I'd eventually return home in the evening, a little bit bodily the worse for wear, but with the little grey cells well stimulated.

We practised together and in twos and threes several times a week. This meant my getting to the nearby town of Haddington by bus. To save my embarrassment of sitting with an uncovered guitar between my knees, my mother made me a travel bag out of an old pair of wine-coloured curtains, which fastened at the bottom by a couple of buttons from an old overcoat. On the journey home on the last bus, someone would invariably ask for a song. I dutifully obliged, of course, but it must have sounded really terrible. Thankfully, the loudness of the bus's engine probably covered my offerings, but it provided an experience I don't regret or will forget. Below is a photo taken at the Legion, published in the local newspaper.

Graham Cassie, John Logan, Nita Cowley Alec Young, Derek Dewar and Jim Douglas.

One Sunday morning, I heard Louis Armstrong on "Two Way Family Favourites" and my musical world took a new direction. I think the song was "Blueberry Hill", but if I am unsure of that, I am doubly certain that I wanted to hear more and to this end, must have driven Wattie mad in my desire to know all he knew about him and other stars of the jazz world. He told me of the early days in New Orleans where Louis, of course, was born and from where the music spread to St Louis, Chicago, Kansas City and, eventually, world-wide. So my appetite was well whetted! There were a few records in the house, stored in an old wooden cheddar cheese box, which my Grandmother played occasionally on a wind-up gramophone. They consisted of a few classical and operatic discs, a fair number of Scottish recordings by Harry Lauder and Will Fife and bagpipe music and a few nuggets of pure gold. I discovered three in particular. They were a banjo solo by a Mr. Bert Bassett with the now unacceptable title of "Coon Slumbers", Ella and Louis' "Frim Fram Sauce" and a Paul Whiteman offering of "When Day is Done". Scratchy but wonderful! Even better, Wattie was the proud owner of a 'radiogram' which not only played records but also featured a good quality radio receiver. He had collected some jazz recordings himself, but the icing on the cake was the ability to tune in to foreign stations such as Radio Luxembourg and Hilversum, which presented a fair number of jazz 'classics'. I was introduced to such early inspirations as Count Basie, Benny Goodman, and Les Paul.

I couldn't get enough. I was still 'skiffling' but my musical aims and dreams were heading in a different direction. Rock'n'Roll in the form of Bill Haley and the Comets, Elvis Presley with Scottie Moore on guitar, Tennessee Ernie Ford and the Platters still played a huge part in my embryonic musical education, but the wizardry of Les Paul and Charlie Christian was taking over and inspiring my guitar-playing ambitions.

Ken Colyer and Chris Barber were already

making an impression on British ears, more and more abandoning their skiffling successes to return to the New Orleans revival that George Webb and Humphrey Lyttelton had pioneered in London, Bob Barclay likewise in Leeds, the 'Merseyssippi' Band in Liverpool and Sandy Brown and John and Archie Semple in Edinburgh.

Chapter Two

"Skiff to Riff"

Jack,   Kimber,   Jim,   Bobbie,   Pete,   John

I was, as I said in my opening paragraph, still at school, of course, studying for my "Highers" which strangely enough did not include music. In the fourth year, you could drop the subjects less of interest to your plans for the future and concentrate on those which might eventually lead to a career. My main idea at the time was to emulate another uncle, this time on my father's side, and become an architect. More and more, I found myself in the art room with various other students from different years and which was often full of students from first and second- year classes. To preserve text books, most schools had insisted on pupils wrapping them with a covering of brown paper. It won't be a surprise for you to learn that the brown paper I had wrapped around my text books was covered in drawings of imaginary, longed-for guitars. I was one of two from my year sharing the studio with two from the year above us. One of those was the aforementioned Pete Kerr. I had latched on to him immediately and soon found we had a lot of common interests, including pipe bands and jazz. My drumming father had been a lead "tipper" in the Royal Army Medical Corps, but also occasionally indulged himself in a little dance band work. On spotting my interest in the art of percussion, he had taken it upon himself to set me on the right path, by teaching me some rudimentary rolls and "licks" and by encouraging me to join a pipe band. As it happened the father of one of my biker mates was about to form a Boys' Brigade Unit and when I heard it would include pipes and drum instruction I joined like a shot. So, by the time I discovered that not only did Pete draw pretty well, he could also play the bagpipes. The idea of forming a school pipe band with two other pipers and myself delighted the headmaster, Mr Anderson by name. He proudly presented us on all sorts of occasions, including a performance in the Massed Schools Pipe Bands display at Edinburgh Castle. As time passed, I found out he was also inspired by Monty Sunshine and, more substantially, Benny Goodman, in learning to play the clarinet. Although neither of us knew it at the time, our futures were to be intertwined from then on. As our friendship blossomed, he introduced me to music of both genres. We formed a jazz band with the addition of Pete's future brother-in-law, Kimber Buglass, who had been blowing a bit of jazz in his National Service Royal Air Force Unit and had recently been demobilized, complete with trumpet, boundless enthusiasm and most importantly for me, a chord book of standard jazz numbers.

At first I had wanted to play drums but Pete presented me with two reasons why I should play guitar and eventually, reluctantly, a banjo, which I received as a permanent loan from an enthusiast fan, after he had retrieved it from an attic somewhere. His reasoning was simple in its eloquence. The main point was, of course, that there were several drummers asking after the position and no chord men, piano players or otherwise, in our less- than-jazz-oriented vicinity. With the help of Kimber's chord book, in which the songs were, fortunately, for the most part, fundamentally correct, I soon learned a few basic tunes. As the more astute of you will have seen from the photograph of the "Tynesiders", I had progressed to amplified guitar thanks to the part-time work I had found at the local village butcher's shop and from grouse-beating, potato harvesting and the like. Being the only one of us in the Skiffle group ambitious and inventive enough, with the help of the bravado of youth, I had been promoted to the role of the group's "Denny Wright", with all due respect to the great guitarist.

It had proved to be a natural progression from "Skiffle" to "New Orleans Jazz" for the likes of Ken Colyer and Chris Barber, with the result that our first rhythm section consisted of three members of the "Tynesiders". Derek started on washboard, eventually progressing to drums and John brought his bass contraption. The two-man front line of Pete and Kimber proved perfectly adequate while we spent hours learning tunes and generally improving our limited techniques. John decided he was just not going anywhere with the oil can so, one afternoon, after he had finished work as a printer at the local newspaper, the "Haddingtonshire Courier" we caught a bus to the capital, where he purchased a double bass he had had his eye on. Nobody had warned us how difficult it was to transport a double bass on a double decker bus and, in fact, we only managed it by standing on the open platform at the rear and holding on to the vertical pole which assisted alighting and disembarking.   The ensuing problems to passengers getting both on and off and the looks we got from them, became a source of amusement among the chaps for weeks after, but we managed somehow and the relief on the conductor's face when we got off is still in my memory. (At this point, I am reminded of a terrible joke which was a favourite of the late pianist, Bert Murray: "As the bus conductor said to the armless, legless chap at the bus stop, 'How are you getting on, then?'")

But I digress!   What of a trombone player? Our wagon would indeed be un-roadworthy without a tailgate! The answer was again just around the corner. I somehow remember that a mate of a mate of a mate had heard of a mate who was enthusiastic and had a trombone. Actually, in reality, Jack Blair was a fellow enthusiast and a good friend of Pete's. He answered the call to become, with the addition of singer Nita Cowley, the last pieces in the jigsaw puzzle that we were trying to put together to form our band.

But it would need a name, of course. At this stage there was no leader and, although Pete would eventually take the mantle on his more than adequate shoulders, we were all in this adventure together and decided a name like "Climax" or "Stompers" sounded more authentic to our dreams and aspirations. After several suggestions, including the exotic "Clam Bake Six", almost borrowed from Tommy Dorsey (although the nearest indigenous shell fish had given their name to the nearby coastal town of Musselborough), we decided on a play on words on the name of our home town of Haddington. We decided that "The Hidden Town Dixielanders", based on the facts that the town was in a sort of valley and the Southern States of America had donated their name to the music we were desperate to play, would be the most apt.

Soon we felt ready to unleash our sound on the ears of the unsuspecting public. We had held a few "private" auditions and received enough positive feedback to encourage us to organize a dance. With the help of an advert in John's paper, the "Haddingtonshire Courier", together with some ticket sales from advertising by obliging shop owners and general word of mouth, we filled Ian Glass's school bus and set off one Saturday evening to Innerwick Village Hall, about ten miles or so from Haddington. To my concern, the first thing I saw was a sign proclaiming:

DANCING WITH TACKETTY BOOTS PROHIBITED. RUBBER SOLES ALLOWED.

The evening proved successful anyway, boots or no boots and led to several re-bookings. Encouraged by our success and driven by my fellow villagers, curious to find out what this spotty-faced, embryonic-beard-growing, guitar-owning, hip-talking teenager was up to and whether he was any good or not, I asked Pete to approach the organisers of the Saturday night 'Hooley' held in a God-forsaken shack known as the Long Yester Village Hall situated in the foothills of the Lammermoors, where my grandfather had conversed with his ovine charges. We were accepted as a sort of audition, as long as we shared the evening with a regular Scottish Country dance band. I seem to remember that, eventually, when the hall filled up after the pubs closed, it wouldn't have mattered what we played as long as the inebriated dancers could somehow or other fit a 'Nips o' Brandy', 'Dashing White Sergeant' or 'Eightsome Reel' into the tune we were playing. The more adroit followers of Terpsichore had no trouble at all of course when we announced 'Tiger Rag' or 'Basin Street Blues' as a Quickstep or

Foxtrot. It was a success anyway, we were re-booked and, as a result, climbed one step higher on our ladder to fame and fortune, even if Long Yester was hardly on the average agent's booking lists!

Gradually the band and its repertoire improved. Gigs became more frequent and widespread, ranging from dances to pub events and even United States Airforce ten-cents-a-drink nights (when everything cost just ten cents and where we discovered our first real hamburgers). Derek, who was finding it difficult to do all the gigs because of employment demands, was replaced by a more experienced drummer, 'Wee' Bob Sandie, who had had amateur experience playing in pipe bands, but whose future lay in chemistry. More about that later! We eventually came to the notice of Duncan McKinnon, who supplied bands for dances in a network of dance halls throughout the Border Counties, even as far south as Newcastle upon Tyne. He gave us gigs as a support band with such attractions as Mick

Mulligan's 'Magnolian' Jazz band, Bob Barclay's Yorkshire Jazz Band and Nat Gonella's 'Georgians'. We were booked to play at the Fountainbridge 'Palais-de-Danse in Edinburgh on the evening of Pete Appleby's famous drum solo, when George Melly tripped the switch to set the revolving stage into action, much to the delight of the audience, who were treated to the arrival of the rest of the Mulligan band playing cards while the shouting, swearing drummer disappeared from sight! One of the 'bouncers' on the door that evening was a certain Tom Connery who was to later gain fame and fortune as an actor after changing his first name to Sean! I think "Drunken Duncan" (there was always a bottle of whisky included in the fee) as he was affectionately known, saw us as an eventual addition and perhaps, rival, to the successful, Glasgow-based "Clyde Valley Stompers" as another draw to help promote his "Border Dances" organisation. We were an important attraction on his circuit by this time, appearing at his flagship venues in places like Kelso, Dumfries, Eyemouth and Haddington 'Corn

Exchange' itself.

Things went from strength to strength. "Carroll Levis Discoveries", an early "X Factor", came to Edinburgh and we entered and won! One of the outstanding memories for me of the occasion was meeting and shaking hands with the young Jackie Collins, who was his 'glamour-girl' for the shows. The prize was a trip to London to record a tune for his "Winner's Showcase" or some such programme, where I was met off an early-morning train by my uncle Jake, who came to the afternoon performance at the "BBC Playhouse" in Northumberland Avenue. In the evening, after the nerve-racking recording, he showed me the West End, taking me to a pub in Frith Street, where I sampled "Light and Bitter" for the first time and ending up listening to the Bruce Turner 'Jump' Band at what was then known as 'Jazzshows Jazz Club' at 100 Oxford Street. On the return trip by the midnight train, to help the journey and appease a toothache I was just about enduring, (any excuse will do!), R Sandie produced a gripe water bottle full of pure alcohol which he 'dispensed' by teaspoon, one per bottle of real 'Coca-Cola' with all its original ingredients. Wow!

A few weeks later, I had the euphoric, out of body, experience of hearing myself on radio for the first time. The tune was either "Alexander's Ragtime Band" or "Down by the Riverside" or some such well-known favourite.

We appeared in a concert at Edinburgh's Usher Hall, accompanying the famous sons of the city, Sandy Brown and Al Fairweather and travelled to Glasgow and Dundee to appear at jazz clubs. We even drove all the way to Aberdeen to support Joe Harriot at the Beach Ballroom and play for Duncan's Northern counterpart, Bert Ewan at his jazz clubs in Inverurie, Huntly and Mintlaw.

Gigs came thick and fast, but so did personnel changes. Kimber decided to concentrate on his job as a joiner and resigned, to be replaced by a future sub-editor of "The Scotsman", Alastair Clark. Bob became a pharmacist and was replaced by Edinburgh drum legend, ex-"Nova Scotia Jazz Band" founder member, George Crockett and Ken Ramage joined on trombone for a few months before joining Charlie Gall in Germany. Ken was replaced at various stages by George Oswald (who became an arranger for Basil Kirchen and Ted Heath), Archie ("Old Bailey") Sinclair and, finally, the great John McGuff, who shared his appearances with us and the Hawick-based "Wool Town Jazz Band". We added a pianist, a student doctor called Bob McDonald, who brought a fine knowledge of the works of Fats Waller with him.

At some stage we went into a privately owned small studio in a department store on the North Bridge in Edinburgh, to record a couple of singles published by the owners of the store on their "Waverley" label. I remember one of them was "Coney Island Washboard", on which I offered a youthful, adenoidal, dialectic vocal and an embryonic banjo solo. None of us had recorded previously, so we had reached another stepping stone in our ever-widening lifestream.

All this time, I was still at school. Half of my mind was divided between lessons and adolescence, while the remainder became totally infatuated with jazz and the band. Things were difficult at home. My father, who, for some financial demeanour in his employment, had been given a short prison sentence and was therefore not contributing to the family income. I brought a little extra into the coffers from gigs, but we were pretty strapped for cash. I considered two offers I had received, namely a boarding Scholarship at Fettes College and an apprenticeship with Sir Basil Spence's Architectural organisation. After careful deliberation, I decided on something much less grand, but nearer home. An Edinburgh-founded company, "Castle Wynd Potteries" had re-established their business in my village of Gifford, after discovering a source of terracotta clay in the area. On looking for staff, they approached me to offer an apprenticeship. So, for the princely weekly wage of two pounds, thirteen shillings and four pence, I became a trainee potter. I did quite well and learned quite quickly. I still own the first pot I ever threw, which is a source of nostalgia and pride to me to this day. Staying in Gifford, of course, meant I was able to carry on with the band!

Working on the potters' wheel had certainly put my life in a spin, if you'll excuse the pun. I learned about different clays and glazes, made Plaster-of-Paris moulds which I filled with a liquid clay called "slip" and discovered the effects of temperatures on glazes in the kilns. I visited Stoke-on-Trent, enrolled in Edinburgh College of Art as a night student twice a week and in general was feeling that my future was now settled. I even bought a 1938 Morris 8 "Tourer" from my boss's brother to replace the clapped-out Excelsior motor bike with two-speed tank-mounted gear shift and forever-needing-replacing chain I had bought from a mate for a fiver and set about learning to drive. All this time I continued to play with the band.

Boy, oh boy did I have fun with that old car! The first thing facing me before I could get behind the wheel was to get it roadworthy. It had been explained to me that incorporated in the engine was the mounting bracket, a thin plate in the shape of a wishbone with appropriately placed holes to allow the flowing of oil and water around the engine and fixing points of anchorage to the chassis., which sat towards the front of the side valve engine, just behind the timing chain. I know all this because I had to take one out of an engine in a car in a breakers yard one afternoon. How naïve I was!   I had been directed to Bernard Hunter's car-breakers yard in Seafield, a links suburb of Edinburgh, where I turned up one Saturday afternoon, dressed to go out on the town afterwards and where, after having an engine with its mounting plate intact pointed out to me, was handed some spanners and told to help myself. Hours later with all ideas of a good time in Edinburgh dispelled by frustration and hunger, I caught a bus home with the acquired article wrapped in newspaper under the armpit of what had been, in the morning, a decent suit. Fortunately, Peter, the village's Polish mechanic in my local garage, undertook to replace it in my vehicle, which involved his setting the timing, only charging me enough for a packet of cigarettes and I was up and running. The police road presence around my neck of the woods was, apart from a village bicycle-mounted bobby, almost non-existent in the days of my youth and I constantly drove alone covered only by a provisional licence without any real fear of being pulled up. I was taxed and insured, but the latter would probably have been voided in an accident. I even took my partially-sighted granny to visit her brother, who lived a few miles away, on a dark winter evening with hopelessly inadequate, dynamo-driven, lights. At one stage in the journey, I almost dumped the carriage, its passenger and driver in a ditch when I failed to negotiate a sharp bend in the road. On another trip to watch a professional band performing at the fishing village of Eyemouth I came out at the end of a concert to be greeted by a flat battery and ending up being jump-started by none other than the legendary

Bobby Mickleborough, to struggle home with the help and kindness of the 'man in the moon' with, happily, no further episode. What fun indeed!

But the "Horns of Dilemma" were about to poke me right between the eyes!

Around 1954, Harold Pendleton had formed his National Jazz Federation with great success in London. It spread north of the Border and its Scottish representative began to show an interest in "Pete Kerr's Dixielanders", as we were now known. The personnel had yet again somewhat changed to include singer Frances Day's accompanist, pianist Alex Shaw, Ian Brown on bass to replace John Logan, who had retired to start a family and trumpet player Andrew Lauder, who replaced a recently promoted to sub-editor, Alastair Clarke.

The bombshell dropped in the offer to turn professional and undertake a two-month engagement in Germany! I was eighteen years old and by a couple of years the youngest member of the band. What about my future as a potter? If there was no work to return to, could I carry on my apprenticeship? How would my mother take the news and react if I decided, as virtual "head of the family", to go so far away and to Germany, of all places. The money on offer, although not fantastic, was reasonable and I would be able to live well enough and still send money home. I put it to my boss who, with great disappointment, said he would, reluctantly, not stand in my way but couldn't hold my job for economic reasons and a replacement would have to be found as soon as possible if I did decide to leave.

God bless my mother! She must have been devastated by my news after all the disappointments she had endured in a troubled marriage. After a lot of thought and discussion with the other band members to ensure they would look after me, she tearfully put her arms around me and wished me all her love and hopes for my future. My brother Ian had joined the Royal Air force as a boy entrant and my other siblings were still at school. My estranged father, now released back into society, had tried to rekindle his relationship with his family to no avail and moved out of the home for good, taking a job as a medical orderly in Edinburgh. So, after changing the band's identity once more, we set off on the long road and rail trip to Cologne as "Pete Kerr's Capital Jazz Band", complete with new passports, tartan jackets and shirts, high excitement and an uncertain future.

Chapter Three

"Pretzels und Bier"

I am still not sure what nationality John Marshall was. I can tell you he sounded American but, with his Aryan blonde, short-cropped hair, he could easily have passed as a leftover from Hitler's "Master Plan". He was, I believe, homosexual and, indeed, surrounded by "pretty", young German "helpers". I felt distinctly uncomfortable at the mandatory handshake and detected a slight glimpse of querulous interest in his searching, blue eyes. (This will sound homophobic by today's standards, but this is the way it was in 1960.) His environment was a circuit of Jazz Clubs in the cities of Cologne, Frankfurt and Mannheim and I believe he had an interest in the Star Club in Hamburg, where the "Beatles" had found their direction. He called his empire "Storyville Jazz" after the famous district in New Orleans.

We arrived in Cologne *Haupt Bahnhoff* on the morning of the first day of December nineteen hundred and sixty. Not one of us spoke a word of German, just as the "hausfrau", Sophie Schreiner, who was to be our landlady for the rest of the month, had not a word of English. This period would of course include Christmas and "Hogmanay." Our "digs" were in two adjoining rooms - four beds in one and three in another, with a connecting door between and a bathroom/toilet with no frills, on the side. The beds were almost adjacent to each other, meaning some of us had to climb over them to reach our appointed sleeping station. I haven't mentioned that I considered myself to be a "Beatnik" at this time, following on from a drainpipe trousered, drape-jacketed "Teddy Boy" and had knitted a knee-length navy V-necked jumper to wear over my white, detachable-collared, blue striped shirt and knitted, black "Slim Jim" tie, narrow black trousers and boots. Oh yes, and I had let my hair grow and I didn't wash much! What a twit I must have looked to the conservatively dressed German jazz fans and an embarrassment to the band, I have no doubt. It didn't last long! Without due ceremony, on the third morning of our stay, I was grabbed by two of the heftier members of the orchestra and dumped, clothes and all, into a pre-drawn bath. I remember thinking how nice it was to feel clean again and my whole approach to personal hygiene changed, as my recent past history disappeared with my aspirations of Bohemia, down the plughole.

The gig rules were 8.30pm until last customer, which sometimes meant three in the morning. My fingers, having spent so much time in water and liquid clay in my job at the pottery, were soft and tender and, before the end of the first week, started to bleed. But there was no respite. I was the banjo / guitar player and therefore held the distinguishing trump card differentiating our style between "Traditional" and "Mainstream" jazz. I was also the vocalist! *Gott im Himmel! Bitte, der Deutches hilpfen!* With careful housekeeping and nursing, my fingers hardened and the discomfort dissipated. From that day to this, my fingers have never given me any trouble and, even after a lean spell gig-wise, soon harden up.

We were thankfully not alone on the bill, however. The real draw was the cabaret star. We were there for dancing mostly although, after a couple of weeks, we had built up a small fan base of local "jazzers" with whom we communicated in our non-existent German and their "Pidgin" English.

Our December 'Star' was the legendary Latin American percussionist and singer, famous from his time with the John Dankworth Orchestra, Frank Holder. He relied on our rhythm section quartet of piano, bass, drums and a guitar player, who were not paid for their extra efforts.

Now might be an appropriate time to relate a story of a famous poster advertising the aforementioned orchestra. The "Clavioline", a sort of electric piano attached to the regular instrument's keyboard, was all the rage at the time. The singers in the orchestra were, of course, Frank and the great Cleo Laine. The poster read:

"The John Dankworth Orchestra,
featuring Frank Holder on the Cleolaine!"

I befriended a young trumpet player named, I presume, Bismarck Paffrat, "Bix" to his friends, with whom, I am sorry to say, I have lost contact. He showed me great kindness in helping me to learn elementary *Deutsch* and by inviting me to his home to sample his lifestyle and the "German Way". With natural reservations from its being only a decade or so after the War, (I promise not to mention the War again!) I enjoyed his company immensely. I have to say that the reservations were all on my side of the fence, fuelled by the bigotry that "all Germans are the same." How wrong can you be? We all have red blood under the skin, as Fats Waller so poignantly pointed out in his wonderful "Black and Blue". Obviously sensing my homesickness, especially with the Festive Season just around the corner, he invited me to his home on Christmas Day. Cologne was looking beautiful in her Christmas attire, with even the twin spires of the Cathedral shining in anticipation of the approaching Holy event. The mood of anticipation had naturally diverse reactions from some of the guys. Christmas afternoon 1960 turned out to be a special memory for me. "Bix" and I listened to the real Bix and Louis and Django and drank Pilsner and 'Bommerlunder' and ate Sauerbraten, Liebkuchen and Pretzels. *Wunderbar!* The Club had, of course, provided Christmas Lunch for musicians and staff, graced by the owner's presence and most welcome it proved, indeed! I am fortunately able to provide some photographs of this occasion taken with a small "Agfa" camera I purchased from my first German pay packet. This obviously explains my absence from the "snaps" but I am so glad to have been there to take them and they obviously wouldn't exist if I hadn't been so self-indulgent in my efforts to record the experience. Here they all are:

Pete, Waiter ,Frank Holder and wife, Alex, Ian, Andy and George.

I pampered myself with the purchase of some self-indulgent acquisitions: an extended play disc of Django Reinhardt, a wrap-around, button-less, Raglan style, wool overcoat and an outrageous hat, complete with hound's tooth checks and peacock feather. The record and hat proved to be a complete waste of money. Unlike the previously-mentioned camera and the coat, they became prime objects in my fool's paradise. The hat became an unwearable object, open to none-too-silent criticism from the chaps. The former was a complete frustration to me in the fact that, firstly, I wouldn't be able to hear it until I got home and, secondly, when I finally did, it bore no resemblance to the sound I had in my memory of the great man, as it consisted of later recordings than those I was familiar with.

My appreciation of Django had started shortly after the formation of our band. A good, Eddie Condon-styled outfit, the "Royal Mile Jazz Band", held a regular club gig every Sunday evening in a Cafe with the same name on the famous street in Edinburgh which links Holyrood House to the Castle.   Pete and I started to attend the sessions, which were very entertaining and educational but, for me, frustrating in the fact that I had to leave the session at the half-time break in order to catch the last bus home.   The answer to my disappointment came from an unlikely, but most welcome, source.   I had gradually acquainted myself with the guitarist in the band, Alex Marshall by name, who owned the most wonderful instrument I had ever seen or heard, an acoustic "Gibson L10".   When strummed, it "cut right through" the ensemble sound, adding the icing to the cake of an already accomplished rhythm section. As our friendship grew, I was one evening given the chance to hold and strum this amazing guitar. Seeing the delight in my eyes and realising I could play a little he asked me to stay around at the end to continue our chat. I told him of my transport predicament.

"Stay with me, then!",

he offered and, on that invitation, a lifelong friendship was formed between us. He shared a flat with his first wife, (whom, incidentally, I never met) in the Comiston area of the City. Among his record collection were several "Hot Club" albums. On hearing them, I couldn't believe my ears! No one could play a guitar like that! No one except Django Reinhardt, that is! As the weeks passed into months and eventually years, our friendship grew. I still talk to Alex occasionally, although he now resides and runs a band in Santa Barbara in California. In a later chapter, I will cover the intertwining of our lives to a greater extent, but his introduction to me of the wonderful gypsy genius will suffice for now.

Back at the "Storyville Club", Art Blakey dropped by. I photographed him with the chaps showing all the fawning respect he deserved. (I later had great pleasure in playing with him in a jam session in Heidelberg, when the

"Messengers" joined Alex's band in a final thrash.)

New Year's Eve brought another experience. As Scots, we were more inclined to celebrate the turn of the year than the Christmas celebrations. 1960 / 61 brought a new slant to our welcoming in the New Year. In Germany, we were an hour ahead of Great Britain on the clock, which meant we had to raise a glass to absent and present friends twice, sixty minutes apart! Our personal celebration an hour after the Germans' was, for the most part, low key and unobtrusive, with just a small toast and handshake among the chaps. I remember imagining what would be going on at home! How I wished I was there! John McGuff , who was married with a young son, had been experiencing homesickness more than the rest of us and was very disconsolate. When the Continental celebrations kicked in, it was all a bit of an anti-climax for us, saved only by time off and the ability to queue to make a telephone call from the kiosk outside the club when our hour finally arrived and our more humble, personal toasts to each other were complete.

Early the next morning we bade a fond farewell to Cologne and boarded a train bound for Mannheim.

The beauty of the river Rhine and its *Schlossen,* its vineyards and the sprawling countryside on its banks was almost lost on me, indisposed as I was, largely caused by a combination of a 'hangover' and lack of sleep. I have since driven the route several times and even played on paddle-steamer-themed Jazz Festivals on the river's more northern reaches. On this occasion, January the First, 1961, we were welcomed in the buffet car by a friendly barman who offered a complimentary *schnapps* and a selection of cold fare, *frikadellen, wurstchen* and *schnitzels* and the like, which went down a treat and helped to resettle my equilibrium. By the time we reached Mannheim, it was almost back to normal and I was looking forward to seeing the new club and meeting its staff and owner. The name of the club was the "*Schwabinger Kunstler Keller*" and the star was to be Maryland born, saxophonist / clarinettist, Benny Waters. I think we were met off the train and taken by taxis to the club, where we were introduced to Benny and the management, offered a welcome beer and set up the drums, amplifiers and other bits and pieces. When all the arrangements were complete, we headed for our 'digs'.

To say they were even cruder than the Cologne rooms would be chargeable by the 'Trades Description Act.' If I hadn't had the hospitality from Bix in Cologne I would have been tempted to think:

" Zees Chermans are all med!"

Someone came up with: "Welcome to the 'Arabs' quarters!!" I realise that the climate has changed in recent times but I mean no disrespect to either the nomadic Bedouin or the Sheik in his palace. The description is based more on the former, who carries a minimal amount of baggage to furnish his camp. These rooms were just so - basically a camp with nothing but what we carried to furnish it. No soap, no towels, no toilet paper or even towels. We had to provide the lot. We washed ourselves, our clothes and anything else needing lavating, in the same tub in turn and hung them up to dry on a pulley contraption. (Five or so years later, Alex Welsh's band was booked to appear at the club with singer, Beryl Bryden. When we got to the digs, nothing had changed, except that Beryl had arrived early and the bathroom area was festooned by drying elephantine black silk knickers and brassieres, big enough to sleep a couple of sailors on overnight leave!)

There were two rooms this time, separated by a connecting door, which afforded a degree of space, but still no privacy. The larger room similarly contained four beds, with a channel between each pair and a small space at either side. The three beds in the smaller room were almost separated enough to allow access, if legs were lean enough. The rhythm section plumped for the smaller, leaving the front line and yours truly to fight over the four in the other. The dismal bathroom was adjacent to the smaller room.   In the evening or very early morning when the beds were occupied, snoring was the order of the day, sometimes harmonious but, for the most part, discordant.   As the month progressed, John McGuff and I found more to do out of the rooms, in an effort to get away from the squalor of it all and the petty bickering that ensued as a result. We found the local swimming baths, firstly for the joy of just wallowing in the personal indulgence of a private soak in a 'slipper' and later rediscovering the pleasure and exhilaration of attempting a few lengths in the pool.   This became a daily necessity, which passed the time and kept us out of the pubs. I met a girl! Doris was beautiful! With her friend, Ursula, or 'Uschi' in colloquial German, she appeared in the audience almost every night. Every night I became more and more 'twitterpated", to quote Walt Disney, with his kind posthumous permission.

But, even as the course of our, what we believed to be true love ran smooth, other traps were just around the corner. Alex Shaw, our brilliant pianist and father figure to the younger members in the band had a problem. (He was actually known in Edinburgh music circles as "Faither Shaw" with all due reference and respect to the legendary Earl "Fatha" Hines). Alex was a recovering alcoholic! Like many, he had a "Mr. Hyde" side to his kindly "Jekyll". Throughout the month of December in Cologne, with bassist Ian Brown's help, he had controlled his drinking admirably, with only a couple of small beers per evening. But one is too many and a hundred not enough, as the saying goes. Something sparked off something which lit a little fire which, in turn, burst into full flame one evening at the digs. A previous argument had sprung up between the alcohol-affected pianist and the band leader on the band stand one evening when the club was entertaining local dignitaries and the owner.

During one number, Alex was affected by a sneezing fit, during which his upper denture was ejected and propelled on a trajectory which took it in the direction of the VIPs. That night, there was an argument back in the "Arabs' quarters" between the pianist and his so-called minder, bassist Ian Brown, who had promised Alex's concerned sister that he would watch his drinking. During the night Pete was suddenly awakened by an inability to breathe. He discovered the pianist with his face inches from his own and with his hands around his throat, sobbingly pleading for a little understanding. Pete wrestled him off but, in the scuffle, the little finger on his left hand suffered a break. What happened next would have been, and now is, hilarious, if the consequences had not been so serious. Screaming at the top of his voice, Alex emitted:

"My Acme on my Rubber at the end of my Oliver is a bit Rory O'More!"

Perhaps I'd better explain:

At some stage in his career, probably while living in London in his role as accompanist to singer Frances Day, he had come across Cockney "Rhyming Slang". Not knowing more than a few standards, "apples and pears - stairs", etc., he had developed his own vocabulary, which he took even one step further by calling it "McFarlane Lang" - slang of course. So his Acme wringer, finger, on his rubber band, hand, at the end of his Oliver Twist, wrist was Rory O'More, sore! Great fun, but I ask you?

It didn't stop with Alex though! We all had a go at inventing our own rhymes including, at a later date, a certain Ron Mathewson, the wonderful Shetland bassist, who was at that time as naive in real life as he was gifted in music. I wasn't around for his first epic utterance, unfortunately, but had it on good authority from the late tenor saxophonist Jack Duff, with whom the bassist was working, that it went along these lines: Ron, a little baffled by all the rhyming, suddenly "fell in":

"Ah, I get it! You just think of a word that sounds like the real one!"

Jack waited with growing anticipation and wasn't disappointed:

"I don't half fancy a Tommy Dorsey!"

said the bassist. After fruitless, careful mind- searching for a suitable rhyme, Jack asked:

"What's that, Ron?"

"A cup of coffee, of course!" replied the bassist.

Later, he was reported as having informed everyone he was going to get a "Tom Thumb" - a gun of course! I digress!

After the fracas, according to Pete, the wounded pianist sloped out of the flat into the night. Returning the next morning, finger in a splint administered by some nuns in a convent he had stumbled upon, he informed us he was going home. My job description changed, of course. We replaced Alex with a young local pianist, who was not too bad but, unfortunately, not in the same league as "Faither". A lot more responsibility came my way. It was fortunate that Benny was our star in Mannheim and not Frank, who had relied more on the piano-led quartet. Benny played a traditional programme which proved to be exactly what our audiences wanted. Songs like "Sweet Georgia Brown," "Rosetta" and "St Louis Blues" were highlights in his performance as solo numbers. For the rest of the set, he joined in with the band's repertoire, adding a wonderful fourth voice to the front line.

There were fortunately no more incidents for the rest of our contracted month. I learned a great deal and, if anything, became better friends with both Pete and later, Alex, who appreciated my endeavours in different lights.

The dark shadow of returning home to an uncertain future began to hang over all of us in general and me, in particular, with the spectre of saying farewell to Doris. With the exception of John McGuff, who couldn't wait to be reunited with his family and take up his previous job in the building trade, we all wondered what lay in store for us. I had formed some very good friendships in this, the country of our recent enemies and even considered staying, mostly, I must confess, because of my growing interest in my relationship with a certain *fräulein.* Better sense thankfully prevailed, although the train journey home was a mixture of abject misery and alcohol-fuelled hopeful anticipation of the future.

I had learned an awful lot in my two months in the "Fatherland" and hoped that the experience would serve me well as a budding jazz musician in the not-too-clear destiny that lay ahead.

As a footnote to this chapter and to perhaps, hopefully, satisfy the more querulous among you who would like to know what happened to these fine players, I have to report that, apart from Pete, Andy Lauder and myself, they have all "left the building", as the saying goes. I met up several times with Alex and John McGuff at the Edinburgh Jazz Festival in the 1980s. They were still playing superbly. I came across George Crockett in the 1990s, while visiting Ayr with a tribute show called "Let's Do It". George, in his early eighties, was hosting a jazz chat show on local radio and kindly invited me to take part in one.

All three died peacefully when their time came. Not so for poor Ian Brown. The happy-go-lucky, larger-than-life bassist had tried his luck in America in a venture that not only robbed him of his entire wealth but also his marriage and everything he held dear. The poor chap was found hanging from a chair. I will remember him, as I will the others, as a personal friend who meant so much to me, a young boy among men.

Chapter Four

"Trad Mad"

When we arrived back in "Blighty", the "Trad Boom" was in its full majestic, meaningless miasma of mediocrity. Dozens of bands, all thematically presenting themselves in a myriad of mesmerizing, unmusical, pretentious poses, swamped the capital's pubs and clubs and were setting up footholds in towns and cities the length and breadth of the country. Tinnitus sufferers took to hiding in dark, sound-proofed rooms to escape from brassy trumpets, squeaking clarinets, rasping trombones, strident banjos, slapping double basses, rattling rolls on snares and thumping bass drums.

Oh how I wanted to be involved! We thought we would just walk in to an agency and be immediately swamped by offers of gigs - after all, we were well rehearsed, well dressed in our tartan finery and raring to go. On the contrary, it seemed we were extraneous to requirements. There was already one Scottish jazz band in the shape of our old Glasgow rivals, the "Clyde Valley Stompers" (soon to be split in two, when clarinettist, Forrie Cairns, decided to form his own band, taking half of the 'Clydes' with him). Recently "discovered" by Lonnie Donegan and introduced by him to "Pye Nixa" records, the 'Clydes' were going great guns, as the saying is. Faced with this insurmountable barrier, our tartan "Joker" proving to be worthless, some of the guys decided that enough was enough and headed home.

Meanwhile the commercial cacophony roared on. Great jazz classics like the "March of the Siamese Children", "If I Ruled the World",

"Whistling Rufus" and "Bobby Shafto" permeated the sound waves and even made it on to the recently aired television show "Top of the Pops". How I wished I was part of it!

I had no idea that my chance was just around the corner!

Back home with my tail somewhat between my legs, it was time to ponder my uncertain future. The bravado of youth had convinced me that I was heading for fame and fortune, but nothing seemed farther out of my grasp than at that time. I could probably find a few gigs, but the band as such was once again in a state of reformation and once bitten, twice shy was the order of the day. It would be some time before I would undertake anything as rash again. There was no chance of returning to the pottery, my apprenticeship openings had vapourised into the cold night air and it was the wrong time of the year to pick up casual farm labouring jobs.

My mother, struggling with three teenage children and a partially sighted mother was, of course, delighted to welcome me home, but I knew I was just another article in her cupboard of financial problems. Never having had a "proper job", I had no recourse to claim financial help from the Government in any form. It was down to me to sort things out.

Things were to get worse! Pete, disillusioned like me, didn't know in which direction to turn. For the first and hopefully the last time we were like two headless chickens searching for non-existent corn. We scraped and scratched and somehow kept the wolf from the door.

Then it happened! An excited clarinettist turned up at my door.

"Fancy a pint?"

he asked. Once we were ensconced in the bar, he dropped his bombshell:

"Ian Menzies has asked me to join the Stompers, subject to an audition and I am sorely tempted. Fancy a trip to Glasgow on Friday? We'll get a good lunch out of it anyway."

I did and we did! Chicken Maryland to be precise! Pete naturally fitted the bill exactly and within a few days was packing his bags and heading for London, brand new tartan jacket, clarinet and all. I had wished him well while quietly realising that this was probably the end of our little era together. Wrong again, Jim!

What now? On my own musically for the first time, I hadn't a clue. I had bought a guitar in Germany, a "Framus Black Rose" but it was currently impounded by the Dover Customs because I couldn't pay the import duty. My banjo, though still playable, had seen better days, but I had no one to play it with. I sat at home brooding about my future and began to despair slightly. What was wrong with me? Banjo players were working all over the country and I was stuck in a hole in Gifford. My mother knew what was wrong! After a couple of weeks, she came to me and said:

"You had better get your bags packed, you're off to London in the morning. I've arranged a lift with your cousin Bill Brodie on his lorry and you can stay with your uncle Jake in Acton till your luck changes and you get some work."

A couple of days later I found my way to the famous "Blue Posts" behind the "100 Club" in Oxford Street. The first person I spotted was my hero, Diz Disley. I bought myself a pint and sat down at a corner table. As the alcohol took effect, I summoned up enough courage to approach the guitarist. I introduced myself and explained my situation and aspirations.

"Welcome to London! Could you lend me a couple of pounds and I'll buy you a drink?"

he asked. I had arrived with the princely sum of seven pounds to my name but, nevertheless, parted with two of them, fully expecting a return of one sort or another. I have to say that, although I worked many times with Diz and we became good friends, the money was never mentioned again. In the bar, a young trombonist named Cyril Preston had witnessed the whole thing. He approached me to enquire who I was and where I was intending to sleep that night. I explained that I was to meet an uncle in Acton the next day and was just going to hang around till then.

"We can't have that, can we? You had better come home to Streatham with me!"

His offer was the best thing I'd heard since stepping down from the lorry in Barnet a few hours earlier. Recently married and in the process of setting up home, Cyril explained that I would have to take pot luck. I explained how grateful I would be for any comforts. Indeed, there were few! He showed me into an unfurnished spare room with wooden floorboards and a naked light bulb glowing from a ceiling rose. I had just deposited my luggage in a corner when the trombonist returned with some coats and a pillow.

"This is about the best I can do but it's better than the streets",

he said. Then he handed me a book "to take my mind off things" he explained. It was " Nineteen Eighty-Four" by George Orwell! A real cheery book if ever there was one!

So that was my introduction to the London "Trad" scene. Very heartening, I must say!

The next day I met up with my uncle in Acton. Jake shared a room with a Welsh workmate so I had to sleep where I could – on the floor, in the uncomfortable armchair or, at a pinch, with Jake in his single bed.

In all, I I lasted about three or four weeks with Jake. We had a great time together. I looked for employment while he was out doing his own job and I would have some food ready for him when he returned home in the evening, simple as it was. We would have a few pints in the local pubs during the week and go "up West" at the weekend, where we met some friends. Some of these were closet homosexuals (it was still illegal in 1961) which Jake had met while building some steps at the Normandy Hotel in Knightsbridge. Among those were Ray, a Director of an American oil company and the famous hairdresser, Rene de la Rue. There was and never will be any chance that Jake and I could be anything other than heterosexual and our "gay" friends knew that - they simply liked to be in the company of "real" men even though I was still just eighteen and, although no longer a virgin, (but that's another story best left unwritten), well short of final bodily maturity.

I saw Pete with the "Stompers" while I was there. They were appearing at an all-nighter at the Hammersmith Palais. I enjoyed what I heard, but it only served to add to my growing disappointment and envy. After even failing to get an interim job as a conductor on a London bus, I decided that enough was enough and reluctantly got on a bus homeward bound. The story of my applying for a job with London Transport is amusing in its own right, if for no other reason than to highlight my naivety at the time. Having been granted an interview and being asked why I wanted to be a conductor, I replied that I was looking for something to tide me over until I found jazz stardom. I ask you!

After a few frustrating, unsuccessful weeks, I packed my bags and headed north. Back home yet again and still without any direction, I started job hunting. It was April 1961. There was some early-season farm work and a bit of tidying-up with my tree-felling uncle, Wattie, burning branches and cutting logs and the like and I was pleased to earn a little to help out at home.

Just about the middle of April, 1961 the telephone rang and, on answering it, I heard a Glasgow accented voice ask:

"Can I speak to Jim Douglas?"

On replying that I was indeed he, the voice continued:

"Oh Jim, this is Ian Menzies here. How would you like to join the Clyde Valley

Stompers?"

I can't remember much of the conversation after that, but I must have said

"Yes please",

because the next thing I recall is making arrangements to quickly return to London. A whole new way of life was just around the corner!

Chapter Five

"Steaming Jim"

This time I travelled by train overnight, arriving at King's Cross Station in the early hours. I was met by the band bus and whisked off to a hall somewhere in Finchley in North London. The band, including Norrie Brown, the banjoist I was to replace, was there to meet me. I was nervous and excited, but they soon put my mind at rest by telling me that I was there on merit and not just 'nepotism' on the whim of Pete Kerr. The repertoire of the band included two numbers which were special features for the banjo, single string melodies on "Whistling Rufus" and "The Fish Seller". Fortunately, neither proved too difficult for two reasons: firstly, I tuned the strings of my banjo like the top four strings on a guitar and, secondly, after all, I was used to soloing on the latter instrument. All that was necessary was practice and to overcome my nerves on the stage.

There is an album recorded at Worthing, on the south coast, a week or so after joining, which proves I handled them confidently, although the banjo is slightly out of tune on the

"B" string. The picture above is a reproduction of the cover.

For the first few days I stayed in Ian's flat in Walm Lane, in the Cricklewood area of North London. I was made very welcome and soon felt secure of my future for the first time in months. Ian's wife, Janet, as a point of interest, was the reigning Scottish Jive Champion, along with promoter Andy Daisley, of whom more later. I remember some of my first gigs well. The

Hammersmith Palais again, a pub in Morden, a jazz club in Cowley near Uxbridge, the "Refectory" at Golders Green and the "Carfax Ballroom" in Oxford. I also remember my first pay packet of around thirty pounds and what a fortune it seemed. We travelled in Ian's "Humber Hawk', while the instruments were transported in the aforementioned wagon. I had never experienced such luxury. One of my first gigs, for "Pye Nixa" records, was to record a double-sided single of two compositions by the leader: "Black Angus" and "The Big Man". The recording took place in May 1961, two weeks before my nineteenth birthday. After the session, we were invited to have dinner at the "Black Angus Steak House" near Leicester Square by the owners of the chain in recognition of their endorsement. "The Big Man" was indeed Ian Menzies. a tall gangly sort of chap.

I moved into a house in Cricklewood. The Barkers, with their two daughters, lived in a three-bedroomed semi at 53 Prayle Grove. Somehow they fitted in four of the band. Pete, bassist Bill Bain, drummer Robbie Winter and me. There were probably bunk beds but I honestly can't remember. What I do remember is the daughters flirting, and succeeding, with a couple of the guys. Not me, Your Honour! And omelettes! At some stage of my life, I had developed the art of making omelettes and, boy, was my ability abused! Every night on return from a gig, I had omelettes to cook! Ham, mushroom, cheese, Spanish - you name it, I cooked it. The Barker's egg bill trebled overnight after my arrival!

One day, after a lunchtime visit to the pub, I suppose, Pete decided I needed a haircut and set to giving me one. He trimmed my flowing locks to within a half inch of their lives, giving me, after the removal of a top denture and sucking in my cheeks and performing a pecking action, the appearance of a fledgling ostrich. (See photo above.) There exists a DVD of me, taken from a home movie made by legendary drummer, Colin Bowden, on a summer outing to Margate on the good ship "SS Daffodil", fooling around in this guise. I'll only show you it by appointment and with the inducement of several liquid prompters! Someone had at some stage called me "Steaming Jim", which had stuck, a name which, to be truthful, I probably tried to live up to! In my ill-fitting, Buchanan tartan jacket, inherited from Norrie Brown, who was a bit shorter in the arm, my crisp, brand new, white shirt, slim black bow tie, well-tailored trousers and shiny black shoes, I reckoned I was the "bee's knees"! Oh to be Dorian Grey and emerge from my attic looking like that now! My new life was musically fulfilling, financially rewarding, geographically enlightening and totally satisfactory. I was the equivalent of a dog with two tails or the proverbial pig in shit or a combination of both.

When the Barkers and their egg devourers mutually had had enough, I moved into a bed sitter in a house in East Finchley with newest recruit, drummer Robin (Robbie) Winter. We weren't ideally suited to each other (after all he was Glasgow to my Edinburgh!), but our room was idyllic after the claustrophobic existence in Cricklewood. Robbie was a kind and considerate man, a little rough around the edges, but he scrubbed up well. His two drawbacks for me were his heavy smoking and fatty diet, both contributing to the atmospheric conditions in the room, which necessitated open-window fumigation by the landlady during the daytime hours.

On a trip to the north one afternoon, his love of greasy fry-ups nearly did for him. He had been complaining of abdominal discomfort for a couple of days, but it was gradually getting worse and, just outside Hemel Hempstead, came to a head, necessitating finding an emergency phone in a farm. He was rushed to the nearest hospital in Hemel, where he was relieved of the largest, almost bursting, appendix they had ever seen and which they later presented to him in a bottle. I have alluded to the wind output from his peculiar diet, but not mentioned the talent he possessed for controlling it. One afternoon in an hotel in Manchester, he emerged naked from his room walking on his hands and "blowing" the "Colonel Bogey March" in perfect pitched notes. Perhaps the answer to the "Riddle of the Sphincter?"

There was even a beautiful young lady in my life. I met Anne at the "Royal Forest Hotel" in Chingford, in Essex, one Sunday evening. Standing at the front of the audience, she seemed to be watching my every move and to be honest I couldn't take my eyes off her either. She was one of those naturally beautiful girls like Julie Christie or Susannah York, but brunette rather than blonde. She had a wide, sensuous mouth and eyes that you wanted to gaze into forever. Somehow we found each other together in the band break and an easy conversation sprang up between us. Well, this is not a love story and, at this stage of my saga I don't intend taking it down that or any similar path. For a short time, we were close but, of course, very young and sense and sensibility prevailed. We did get as far as an invitation to "meet the parents" though. On the appropriate Sunday, I set off to Silverthorn Avenue in Chingford for lunch with the family. I found the house without too much trouble and, after combing my hair, straightening my tie and buffing my toe caps on the backs of my trouser legs, I rang the doorbell. As the door swung open I was confronted by the face of a goddess.

"You must be Jim!"

An angelic voice emitting from a face equally as sexy and beautiful as that of her daughter welcomed me to her home! How can a hot-blooded young fellow concentrate on roast beef in the presence of two of the most beautiful women he had ever met? Anne and I remained friends, but gradually drifted apart. Not for the first or last time, I think I became too serious about our relationship, where she wanted to be a bit more footloose and fancy free. I was happy to meet up with her again one night, forty years later, on a tour I was involved in with Paul Jones, a tribute to Cole Porter, at an Abbey in Cambridgeshire. Married with grown up children, she still looks wonderful. I do hope she is happy.

The gigs came thick and fast. Sometimes there were even two and, on one occasion at least, three a day. A broadcast or television recording could be followed by a club session in the early evening and an early morning appearance at an "all-nighter" somewhere. I recently discovered one such adventure in an old diary: firstly a Saturday night performance at the 100 Club, followed by an overnight drive to the north west for a Liverpool to The Isle of Man Jazz Excursion on a ferry to and from the island, ending in a session back at the Adelphi Hotel and a mad dash back south to McElroy's Ballroom in Swindon to close an all-night session. I remember that weekend in particular, because of an exhibition of his famous "man, woman and bulldog" by the extrovert singer, George Melly. For anyone of a nervous or delicate disposition, I would suggest skipping the next paragraph, in which I will describe this "cabaret". For the sturdier, more accepting of you, read on at your peril!

"Man, woman and bulldog" was an act of burlesque bravado which necessitated the removal or lowering of the performer's trousers and underpants to present firstly a "gentleman's" masculine genitalia. Secondly, tucking the whole accoutrement between tightly closed legs to portray the appearance of a female pudenda and finally, having turned one's back to the viewers, bending forward to touch one's toes, thus displaying the vision of what might be described as a "bulldog". Grotesque! I recall being totally disgusted but feeling, at the same time, a slight degree of admiration for his audacity. But that was George!

Just on the horizon was the anticipation of a summer season on the lovely island of Arran, off the West coast of Scotland. I had heard from the band members who had been there before what a lovely place it was and how much I would enjoy the concerts. There was also the delightful prospect of having little or no travelling between the three venues and the chance to have a break. Unfortunately, a couple of rain clouds were creeping across my hitherto blue sky.

Before that there were more and more towns, cities, studios, halls and clubs to discover. We appeared at the "Hen and Chickens" in a suburb of Birmingham as well as the Town Hall in the City Centre. The date sheet took us to the "Bodega" in Manchester, the "Trent Bridge Inn" in Nottingham, a club in Stoke on Trent where a butcher's shop next door displayed "urban dairy products", cow's udder and tripe and such and the "Cavern" in Liverpool, in which the ambient temperature was so warm, we stripped to string vests, fashionable then. While there, I bought a beat up old banjo in a junk shop. When I returned home, on closer examination, it turned out to be a "Paramount" style "A" tenor banjo. The vellum was ripped and one of the tuning pegs twisted. I had become adept at lapping drum hoops so this was a doddle. In the days before plastic heads, vellum was the order of the day but it was extremely vulnerable to changes in atmosphere. Many a night I would get home to find my banjo head split, so I kept a few soaking in a basin and I would lap the hoop before retiring to bed. Now I had two banjos, things became much easier. I had by this time rescued my guitar from the Customs and Excise, only to find the neck slightly warped, but playable. Unfortunately, the guitar, especially amplified, was "persona non grata" in the more traditional- based clubs, so I had to limit its appearance to a couple of tunes a night. Even then, at Hornchurch Jazz Club, a promoter, named Claude Spurrin, saw fit to pull the plug of my small amplifier from its socket in the middle of a solo in "St Louis Blues". He got his comeuppance for a different reason later but, in fear of libel, I'll refrain from entering any details here. By the time we set off for Arran, we were all in need of a well-earned break

Chapter Six

"Stormy Seas"

The Isle of Arran off the West coast of Scotland lies immediately East of the Kintyre peninsula and can be reached by ferry from Ardrossan harbour in the Firth of Clyde. Approximately four hundred square miles in area, it is Scotland's seventh largest island. With a population of around four and a half thousand it offers holidaymakers a wide selection of pursuits from fishing, marine and fresh water, golf or just relaxing on its sandy beaches.

111

In the summer of 1961, its three main towns of Brodick, Lamlash and Whiting Bay were highly populated by tourists from all over the United Kingdom and Europe, a large percentage of whom were caught up in the growing "Trad Fad". The "Clydes" were no strangers to the island, having established a regular fan base in and around nearby Glasgow. This year, everywhere was packed! When the ferry carrying the band docked, there were literally dozens of fans and well-wishers to greet us. Having settled in to our digs, I was to share a room with Robbie in a small cottage belonging to a delightful lady whose name I seem to remember as Miss Hyslop and, introduced to a Mrs. Cannon, who was to accommodate the rest of the band members and cook for us, we got ready for the first performance in Brodick town hall.

The first question people asked was where was the pianist? On finding out there was no longer a place in the band for a pianist, due to the current fashion for a banjo-featured rhythm section, the next was if I could replace Norrie with his featured solos?   I was gratified to hear the "Big Man" reply that I was more than able to fill his shoes and what's more I could sing! Yes, you read correctly - I was, along with Malcolm Higgins, featured on several vocals in the band's repertoire.   So, as the evening progressed, I performed my solos and vocals, including a "camp" version of "Sweet Sue", based on the Django Reinhardt version featuring Jerry Mengo, a friend of a certain Monsieur S Grappelli. I need not have worried!   I went down a storm, even to performing an encore with ever more "lisping and mincing".   The band were in convulsions!   "Steaming Jim" had arrived.   Next day was Sunday and there would be two performances!   Lunchtime in Lamlash and an evening session in the third, smallest town, Whiting Bay brought the same reaction. So I had created my monster. Fine, I thought, I can live with that!   I was making a name for myself in a slightly derogatory fashion but, at the same time, furthering   my   musical   techniques   and reputation.   If I put up with this clownish behaviour for the duration of the season on Arran, by the time the band returned to performing on the regular circuit of clubs and pubs etcetera, with daily practice I would be twice the player I had been before. Day after day I drove Robbie nuts with my efforts and, in the evenings, carried on with the cabaret.

Perhaps I am painting a wrong portrait of the band! My share of the performances was a couple of songs a night. The rest included some good hard-hitting jazz from the chaps, led by the remarkable Malcolm Higgins on trumpet and fired by the driving Robbie Winter on drums. We played the standards, of course, but also included swinging versions of "Scotland the Brave", Rachmaninov's "Prelude in C sharp minor", a good brass band tune "Trombones to the Fore" and features by Pete Kerr such as "Memories of You" and "Oh Play to me Gypsy."

Apart from my daily practice, we found time to go fishing and play golf, a good way to keep out of the pubs! On one sea fishing trip I actually caught a sea bass which was presented to Mrs. Cannon and served to us for our evening meal. Life was grand!

Then I got the telephone call.   My uncle Wattie, so often the bearer of good tidings and encouragement, had bad news for me.   My estranged father had been found dead in a bath after some sort of seizure in a medical establishment in Edinburgh where he had found employment as a male nurse. While in the army as a Royal Army Medical Corps private, he had been on duty at Dunkirk. Within months of what must have been a horrendous nightmare, his own nervous system deteriorated in neurotic fashion.   Although non-epileptic, he started suffering from mild fits, especially in baths when the water was hotter than tepid. This is what seems to have happened at his untimely end but, with no one to help, he must have suffered an awful death.   I was told not to return home immediately, as there was little I could do, but would, of course, be expected to be the head pall- bearer at his funeral a week later.

Strangely, after years of not really seeing him, my father and I had run into each other in a pub in Edinburgh only a matter of months beforehand. Actually I knew he would be there from whispers on a grapevine. He was extremely pleased to see me and delighted with my news about the "Clydes". I often wonder if a musician's life would have suited him better. He was certainly a good enough drummer to play with anyone, but fate, alas, had decreed otherwise.

On my return from an acrimonious funeral service, where the two sides of my family bickered with and blamed each other for what had happened, in much the same way as opposite factions at a wedding and what proved to be the last time I saw or spoke with any of the Douglas side, I tried to put the whole affair out of my mind to concentrate on the job in hand. The chaps, though obviously a little shocked at what had occurred, especially to the youngest member of the band, were wonderful to me.

I had settled back into the fold really well and was looking forward to a short flight from the mainland to London to perform in a live television show when the second storm blew up, this time in the literal sense. The day before our scheduled flight, the weather took a turn. Gale force winds and lashing rain battered the island all day and, worse, necessitated the cancellation of all ferry crossings. We were stuck on the island with no hope of getting anywhere, never mind to Prestwick Airport to catch our flight. Enter "Captain Madness", the owner of a twenty-two-foot motor launch.

"I'll take you to the mainland", he said. "It might be a bit choppy, but we should be alright"

Were we mad? Couldn't the TV show be re-scheduled. Seemingly not! The show was "Top of the Pops" or "Trad Tavern" or something of that ilk and we were the top billing. Apart from that, there were pre-paid airfares and other expenses to consider. So we agreed.

At dawn the next morning, we assembled at the harbour, still holding on to our hats and trying to keep as dry as possible, while we battled the elements to batten the drums and double bass to the bulkhead and roof of what looked far too small and fragile a craft for what "Ahab" had in mind. Once everything was considered secure and watertight with the aid of well-secured tarpaulins, we were invited to take our places in the cabin. I found myself wedged between two of the chaps on the starboard side. The skipper introduced a seventh member to the band, a certain "Johnnie Walker", which he placed on the central table within arm-reach. I was already feeling queasy and we were still in the harbour! To add to my feeling of claustrophobia and foreboding, he bolted the door. If I was to end up in "Davy Jones' Locker" at least I'd be dead when I got there, I thought! So off we went, a sick 'steamer' in a steamer piloted by a 'sick' captain!

"They didn't think much t'ocean, t'waves were fiddling' and small."

Maybe in Albert Ramsbottom's Blackpool they were, but here, in the Firth of Clyde, they were at least twenty feet high. I felt like a constituent part of the proverbial cork bobbing on the ocean. Malky, who seemed none the worse for what I considered to be by far the worst experience of my sheltered existence so far, opened the whisky bottle. When it came to me I took a hesitant "swig" and immediately threw up. By the time we had crossed, I had nothing left to bring up and I was shaking like a leaf. We obviously reached our destination or I would not be recalling the nightmare that it was, here and now, but not before rescuing some poor chap clinging to the hull of an upturned catamaran. I seem to remember being unable to dock at Ardrossan and making for Largs instead. There then followed a frantic taxi ride to

Prestwick to just in time mount the steps of a "Viscount", have the instruments stowed in the hold and to take off on a bumpy trip to London.

"If this is 'stardom', they can stuff it up their arses!",

I remember thinking as we neared Heathrow. All of course was "alright on the night" and the show went well.

So that was Arran and a 'peaceful' time was enjoyed by all. In retrospect I did have a wonderful time. There were ladies, of course! The young lady from Paisley with whom I enjoyed walking her dog. Liz from Carlisle with whom I remained a pen pal for years and years and who became quite important in the local Conservative Party. There was also a "scrubber" from "Glesga" who took me for an alcohol-induced stroll in the woods, with the sole intent, on my part, to prove my masculinity and, on hers, to add my name to her list of her carnal collection of banjo players. I don't know what lowly position I graced on her list, but I regret (no I don't, damn it!) that I am definitely on it somewhere, heaven forbid that it still exists!

I have never been back on Arran's soil. One day I have promised myself to return to rekindle the embers of my memories of a wonderful experience on an extraordinarily beautiful island.

Chapter Seven

"New Look Stompers"

In the final days of the Arran booking, a couple of insights into the Menzies' outlook on jazz manifested themselves, sowing the first seeds of doubt into my mind of his *raison d'etre* and perhaps the first inkling of why a successful band had been split in two on more than one occasion. On learning that the Arran project was totally his, noting packed halls for every performance and bearing in mind that we were obviously part of the success, drawing an enthusiastic crowd from all over the mainland, Pete drew the short straw to ask him if a bonus might be on the horizon. The answer came as a resounding negative with the explanation that it was his brainchild and he was stockpiling for the future. But his future was to follow a different path from the one the guys were treading. I had felt for a few weeks a slight dampening in the leader's attitude to performances in particular and enthusiasm for the band in general. It should be remembered that the "Clyde Valley Stompers" were one of the United Kingdom's longest established bands, having been in existence for a decade or so. During this time, Ian had taken over the leadership, endured three major personnel changes and had fought for and bought the band name outright in a Court of Law.

It was not really a surprise then that, when we had our next band meeting, shortly after recording two more singles, "Play to me Gypsy" backed by "Trombones to the Fore" and "Taboo" with what proved to be his 'swan song', "Auf wiedersehn" on the reverse side, he told us of his plans to retire from playing a month later in September 1961. Ian revealed that both he and his wife Janet were just plain tired of the band business and had bought a little guest house on the Island of Jersey to enter into semi-retirement. Being, as I explained, the owner of the name, he had formed a business partnership with his wife and the directors of the Lynn Dutton Agency and had registered it as the "Clyde Valley Stompers and Company Ltd.". Having asked him what plans there were for the future of the chaps he said nothing would change apart from the hiring of a replacement trombone player.

The job of band leader was to be given to Malky Higgins. This was a wrong move in my mind. After all, hadn't we an experienced leader in our ranks already in Pete Kerr? It wasn't long until I was proved right. Malky was a great trumpet player but was just not up to the job. In a matter of weeks, he resigned, citing homesickness and a desire to be with his family back in Glasgow. We agreed that Pete, who was subsequently approached for and had accepted the position of leader was certainly the best man for the job and we would be glad to carry on under him. John McGuff had already agreed to take the trombone "chair" which fitted him like a glove and changed the sound of the band dramatically for the better. Pete required one more addition: he wanted to reintroduce a pianist to the line-up. Although it was agreed in principle, it would have to be put before the committee to discuss financial implications etc. Pete had discussed adding a piano with me on several occasions, probably to decipher my feelings as to whether I felt inadequate or not up to the job. When I said I would be delighted to play alongside a piano again, he even asked if I had anyone in mind.

Things were moving on in the "Trad" scene. Kenny Ball had always, like we had in Germany, adopted a four-piece rhythm section line-up and Acker Bilk had added the wonderful Stan Greig to his ground-breaking "Paramount" band. In fact, before turning professional, we had used several pianists for some time before

Alex Shaw joined. Among them were Edinburgh stalwarts Tom Finlay, future doctor Bob McDonald and Shetland import Harald "Matt" Mathewson, who was also studying in Edinburgh and was the elder brother of bassist, Ron. Several names were mentioned for the "Clyde Valley Stompers" job but one thing was obviously necessary – whoever the successful applicant was, he had to have some tangible thread to or at least a traceable bloodline from Scotland. That narrowed it down a bit. There was Bill McGuffie, of course and Ronnie "Bix" Duff already on the London scene, together with the aforementioned Edinburgh chaps and several more in Glasgow and other cities north of the border. Those who inevitably had the final say in the matter decided that the best way forward was to advertise the position and hold auditions. Well, that was a really good idea, I must say! I knew the Scots were a well-travelled race but I didn't in my wildest imagination realise how much seed they had sown even in the confines of our small Islands. The applicants came from far and near; from islands and highlands and even undiscovered caves and uncharted wastelands in the outer, far flung outposts of the country.

"'My granny's cousin, who married a Scot, has a grandson who can play 'Kitten on the Keys!'"

You know what I'm saying! There was even an application and subsequent audition, one afternoon at the "100 Club", for a "chap" already known on the scene for diverse reasons. Tony Raine or Ted Ram, to use his birth name, was a well-known, (I'll be gentle!) slightly effeminate ragtime pianist, who made no secret of his preference for male company. He 'skirled' his entrance into the audition, clad in complete Highland outfit – plaid, kilt, sporran, skean dubh, cairngorm brooch - you name it, he was wearing it! He even had a "Glengarry" bonnet, complete with eagle feather on his well-coiffed head. (I could tell he was no true Scot – he didn't have dandruff on his shoes!) Ah, if only his musical repertoire had been as eccentric as his garb and his sexuality as far in the opposite direction, we might have done business. In the end we didn't need him and he didn't need us. As the years passed by, he associated himself with a famous pub in London's East End, the "Waterman's Arms", owned by a man of his own sexual persuasion, journalist and broadcaster, Daniel Farson and, later, he made several tours accompanying singer, Beryl Bryden, (she of the large black silk knickers and sailor's hammock-sized brassieres, previously documented).

After several rejected applicants for the post from various musical walks of life, Kirkcaldy-born Bert Murray, who was already domiciled in London, persuaded us that he was the "right man for the job"! Bert had a reputation for being slightly "annoying" when he had partaken of a few beverages, as he was wont to do. He assured us that his anger was usually brought on by musical frustration and was largely behind him, as he had learned "to count to ten". With John McGuff in the trombone chair, after some persuasion from Pete to once more leave the comforts of his home and family and a rested, restored Malky, back as the great trumpeter sideman that he was, Bert joined us just in time to go on a week-long gig to Northern Ireland which turned out to be more frustrating than anything the enigmatic pianist had, or would have, to offer. The Musicians' Union had, for some reason I can't recall (but probably due to the American Union arrangement of tit for tat, musician for musician, band for band etc.), called a strike and were picketing all venues and stopping bands from entering the premises of their engagements. This, of course, affected us and we found ourselves on a paid holiday. Night after night we turned up at the venue to be turned away by gentlemen we certainly didn't fancy getting into an argument with and, even if we had gained admission, we would have been playing to an empty room. In the circumstances, what could we do but spend our working hours in some of Ulster's better known hostelries, such as the famous "Crown" in Belfast? If you have never been there and you find yourself in that city, it is certainly worth a visit. Just opposite the "Europa", the much bombed hotel during the recent "troubles", this marvellous example of Victorian pub architecture, with its gargoyle-topped cubicles and mirrors everywhere, had managed to avoid everything and still proudly offers its wares in the time-honoured tradition.

We spent a fair bit of time there, as you must by now have expected. Bert produced a piano keyboard version of an instrument called a "Melodica" on which he was extremely talented and which he used to put the band into fits of gut-clutching laughter or eye-watering melodic nostalgia. Together with Malky Higgins's fine renditions of Scottish songs, we had a wonderful time. On the way to yet another cancelled gig, we travelled as far south as Warren Point, on the Border between the troubled countries, where we stopped at a marvellous pub. Knowing there was no gig that evening, but fulfilling the contract by getting there, we let our hair down. With no hurry or desire to leave, we found ourselves locked in at closing time and introduced to the delights of "Guinness Triple X", brought up in dusty bottles from the cellar by a beaming, enthusiastic publican.

The only downside to the whole hilarious escapade was that its date sheet coincided with the famous march by the Protestant "Orangemen" through the Catholic environments of Belfast. I found this troubling and disappointing and a little frightening. I may have been born a few miles from the birthplace of Presbyterian reformer, John Knox and, as a youth attended the school named after him in the market town of Haddington, but we had learned to accept all walks of religion by the 1950s, although there was a minority that wouldn't let go and who, to this day, still demonstrate bigotry in football clubs and the like. Ten years later, it was all to come to the boil with the outbreak of the "Troubles", with the Falls Road bombings and the IRA involvement, of course, but the least said about that as far as this book and my feelings towards the fellowship of all mankind, regardless of religion, are concerned, the better.

It's time to dismount from my soapbox and return to more pleasant reminiscences! For a while, things went smoothly - too smoothly. I moved into a room in a terraced house in North Finchley, Number Three, Moss Hall Crescent, owned by a Mrs. Curwood, which I shared with John McGuff. Just off Tally Ho' Corner, it was handy for buses, shops, pubs and restaurants and close to the A1 road to the north, which suited the band itinerary. In the penultimate category, there was an establishment just across from our digs, which became a routine eating and meeting place for the band. The owner, Jean, was from Glasgow originally, but had headed south with her Polish husband to set up a successful catering business. Jean had a younger sister, Betty, who had children of her own but was divorced from their father. I liked her very much and even went out with her a couple of times, although she was a bit older than me. It became almost like family life again. It wasn't working out at Mrs C's and, after an evening of overindulgence on my part and a subsequent accident concerning bed sheets and bodily functions, we parted company. We moved into Jean's on an attic floor for a few weeks until we found something more suitable. While there, I learned a fair bit of the commercial side of cooking by watching Jean's chef husband. One day he said to me:

"I haff hear you like cook omelette so now you haff chance cook big omelette for aiverywan! Zees aigs are on use-by time so must be cooked today."

He pointed to three trays of eggs and handed me a very large frying pan. We started cracking eggs into the bowl of an electric mixer. I counted ninety-two! With the pan warmed up and with his eyes watching me, I cooked a four score and ten ingredient omelette. I dished it up and we got stuck in, about ten of us or so. I can't remember if there were any after-effects like mild constipation or even the opposite, but we survived and lived to tell the tale. Incredible!

While this was going on, Malky had started "playing up" a bit. To be fair, he was probably missing his wife and family once more and maybe even his mates from the previous line up. He started to drink a little too much and even started "dropping a few uppers". One night about midnight he collapsed. I called a taxi and whisked him to Barnet General Hospital, where he was diagnosed as having overdosed and had his stomach pumped. I probably helped to save his life, but I had a feeling afterwards that it was perhaps not what he had wanted and that depression had led him in the direction he had taken. A couple of other incidents, this time drink-related, resulted in his inability to play to his usual high standard. One occasion required Pete, while on a studio date, to make a last minute call for help to the wonderful Kenny Baker. At the same time, clarinettist Forrie

Cairns, who had left the band to form his own, the "Clansmen", was experiencing problems in the same category. I can't recall exactly what happened, but It was obvious that Malky was keen to re-join his family back in Glasgow and this was probably for the best.

Enter twenty-nine-year-old Glaswegian, George Paterson. More of a big band player, George brought a new sound with him. He is a fine player and arranger, having been pop star Englebert Humperdinck's musical director in the 1960s at the time of his hit "Please Release Me." Before all that, he was our trumpeter and singer. It was during his time with us that we were offered and accepted a thirteen-week series on Tyne Tees Television. Every Tuesday night, we caught the sleeper train to Newcastle upon Tyne, arriving at the studio by the waterfront at breakfast time and rehearsing all day. Well, rehearsal was part of it! At lunchtime we visited a pub next door called the "Egypt Cottage" for a pie and a pint with the studio musicians and often some of the stars on the show. Among them were Bobby Vee, who had his "Venus in Blue Jeans" in the charts and who politely declined a drink, but came along anyway. Danny Williams of "Moon River" success did accept a small cider, but it resulted in his forgetting the lyrics of the Mancini classic on his live performance! The show, an evening news and entertainments magazine, was transmitted live between about six-thirty and seven-thirty every Wednesday evening, leaving just enough time to get a couple in at the pub before the light went on! On one edition, I was to sing and play "Wait Till the Sun Shines, Nellie", which involved a banjo introduction and solo. Just before our turn, I decided to sing it without a top denture I wore. Honestly, your Worships, I thought it would be funny. George thought it would also add to the fun if he slipped his strong glasses over my eyes just before the cue from the floor manager. Of course, it was disastrous! I started the whole thing in the wrong key. Mercifully, I somehow managed to find the correct one in the vocal, but I must have been a picture. Funnily enough, no one noticed and it was confined to history without further event.

The best 'sweet and sour' story of the series came halfway through. After the show, we always went back to the pub until closing time and a taxi whisked us off to the station to return once more on the midnight sleeper. It was Robbie Winter's birthday. He decided to celebrate it fully by choosing Newcastle Brown and whisky chasers as his tipple. By the time the taxi arrived he had downed THIRTEEN! By the time we arrived at the platform, he was almost unconscious between a pair of us. As we struggled to get him on the carriage, he somehow wriggled out of our grasp and fell between the steps and the platform, suffering several cracked ribs in the process. He must have been in agony but, fortunately, 'passed out' for the entire journey. We got him to hospital in the morning, but what a birthday! I'll bet he never forgot that one, God rest his soul.

On New Year's Day 1962, Pete married his lovely wife, Lori. I was delighted to be invited to be his Best Man, a role I undertook with great pride. As a gift, Pete gave me a signet ring. (I still have it, but it now proudly adorns the ring finger of my son William's right hand.) The next day, George followed suit and wed his first wife, Ruth in Glasgow. It seemed that weddings were in the air. Not for me! I had too much living to do!

George lasted on trumpet for about six or seven months, before deciding he had had enough. To be honest, several arguments and one incident (which I don't intend to dwell on) had caused a slight rift between him and some members of the band, including the leader. The parting of the ways seemed the best outcome. His replacement was one of the best "Dixieland" trumpet players ever to grace these islands. Before that, history intervened in the shape of Dean Kerr, former trumpeter with the "Clydes", who now resided in Southend-on-Sea and was on the board at Selmer Musical Industries.   No relation to Pete, he brought a different sound to the band for a few weeks. He would have been great for the band, but just couldn't find the time to join. I enjoyed his driving playing and good company. As good as Dean was, his permanent replacement - well, for a few months at least - was superb.

Ulster-born Joe McIntyre had followed Kenny Ball into the Sid Phillips commercial jazz organization, where he had combined his natural talents with Sid's arrangements to perfection.

Joe came from a musical family. His cousin, Gay led a successful "show-band", touring all over Ireland, playing all sorts of music. As a side-line, Joe was learning Irish jigs on the fiddle, dancing as he played. He was a short man, with a huge talent and a heart to match. His wife, Mairead, was from the Guinness family. (For those not in the know, the Guinness family are famous for some sort of alcoholic stout ale!) The whole band were totally elated when he agreed to join.

Joe brought all sorts of musical ideas with him. He, of course, knew the Dixieland classics note-perfectly from his time with Sid (who was an absolute stickler for musical correctness) but he also had tunes that were screaming in his head to be let out, which the famous society clarinettist deemed unsuitable for the orchestra's repertoire. "Yes, We have no Bananas!" was such a number, played in a way the composer never dreamed of and "When Irish Eyes Are Smiling" another. All the bands in the "Boom" were desperate for tunes to follow the Kenny Ball "circus parade" of top ten hits, which seemed to flow in an unending stream of watery jazz-based rivulets. Acker Bilk was slightly better, in my opinion, inasmuch as he at least included a degree of honest jazz in his offerings. What "Siamese Twins" have to do with jazz beats me. Maybe there is a conjoined pair of saxophonists or trumpeters somewhere in the world but I have never in my fifty odd years of following the art form, heard of such a duo. However, of course, we were no exceptions! With the dual purpose of achieving both fame and financial gain, we were right "up for it!"

So let's get at it! Let's have a band meeting to pool ideas! Let's book some rehearsals ASAP! I can't claim sole responsibility for suggesting "Peter and the Wolf", but I do remember mentioning it as a possible piece, (born out of my memories of a school performance of Prokoviev's classic, see the photograph in chapter One). at a concert somewhere. Whoever did have the last say is unimportant now, but it seemed like a good idea to have a go at it. We combined to head-arrange it, with a large part, especially the chordal structure, coming from Bert and the front line harmonies from Joe, Pete and John, but we all put in our pennyworth and the result was what went on to reach number eleven in the hit parade. It was recorded by "Parlophone" records and engineered by George Martin who, of course, oversaw the "Beatles" hits. I think it proved to be one of the better efforts from the output of the "Trad Boom".   Its success did bring extra exposure, such as television appearances on shows like "Val Parnell's Star time", "Thank Your Lucky Stars" and the "Morecambe and Wise

Show"

On the "B" side, we presented a jazzed-up version of the old Scottish classic, "Loch Lomond." This was used by Scottish Television as the introductory and closing theme for their daily news magazine. It must have paid the limited company a fair amount in royalties, but the musicians never saw any of it. All in all, the rewards we received for selecting, arranging and recording a top twenty hit were less than encouraging, to say the least. The rodents were beginning to give off a pungent aroma.

Financial matters aside, everything was running pretty smoothly. There were plenty of gigs, to which we were driven in a hired coach by a gentleman called Ted Putt, an apt name if there ever was one. We had abandoned the lurid tartan jackets in favour of the smart, tartan-lapelled, heather-coloured suits you see in the above photograph and the chaps all got on well with each other. We even managed to keep Bert's idiosyncrasies to a minimum, apart from a couple of occasions when he nearly got us into the literal excrement. The first was at Bridgnorth in Shropshire, where we played at a boozy afternoon concert at the Royal Air Force station. Finished by about five, we found our digs in a small hotel and went "out on the town". We all ended up the worse for wear including Bert who, as we approached and opened the door of the hotel at around midnight, suddenly exclaimed:

"I think I'm going to be sick!"

He rushed along the corridor to where the single toilet was, wrenched open the door and threw up all over the bewildered landlady, who was taking her nightly constitutional!

Bert in his own way followed Alex Shaw in taking me under his wing musically and I showed my appreciation by listening intently to his ideas and beliefs. He went even further in cementing our friendship by inviting me to Sunday lunch with his charming wife, Marion and their over-indulged poodle, Heather, in their flat in Canonbury, near Highbury Corner in Islington. We would have a couple of pints in a local pub, where there was a lunchtime jazz session and, after a well-cooked, beautifully- presented lunch, relax to the music of Eddie Condon and Bert's particular favourite, (he was also quite adept on trombone), the wonderful Jack Teagarden.

These were special afternoons, which portrayed the real Bert Murray and belied the "Mr Hyde" that emerged when he drank too much, the belligerent little sod most people thought he was and his delusional belief that his erratic behaviour portrayed him as a bit of a character. I believe, although he never divulged as much, that his Catholic upbringing had been compromised by the lack of children, which I believe from my own experience from my first marriage to a lady of that faith, to be a necessary expectation by that particular creed. Having remounted my soap-box, I will quickly state that I believe too much pressure is forced upon members of that particular sect to adhere to that requirement and, having stated my opinion, I will jump straight off it again. What I believe or do not believe has no bearing on this recollection of generally happy times.

Before closing my short portrait of Bert, I will recall one more event.

We had returned from some job or other and were dropping the pianist off near his home at Highbury Corner. Most of us had got out to stretch our legs, including Pete and his lovely wife, Lori. Some heated drunken words were exchanged between one of the chaps and myself, which resulted in my using some, at the time, unsavoury words, describing a certain part of a lady's anatomy and others. Pete took natural offence to this outburst within Lori's earshot and asked me to stop swearing, whereby I responded by shouting:

"I've used worse words in front of better women than her!"

Ouch! The next thing I knew I was pinned to the railings and deservedly receiving a couple of whacks to my body. When I calmed down, I saw Bert crying quietly and begging us to stop. He was really just a big softy at heart. As

annoying as he could be, I liked him very much.

Chapter Eight

"Horns a Plenty"

For a few months, we were 'rulers of the roost', riding on the success of our hit record, touring all over the country, making new friends and meeting old ones, playing to packed theatres and clubs and appearing on radio and television almost weekly. I was even interviewed as the youngest member of the band for a broadcast to Australia and remember being horrified at the sound of my highly- accented voice on the playback. The band seemed settled at last.

On one trip however, a strange conversation sprang up about heart attacks - not, you might think, a subject too close to the thoughts of a band of healthy young guys in the prime of their lives. It transpired that both Joe and Bert endured frequent dreams in which they suffered an attack, but survived. It may seem relatively narrow-minded or even bigoted on my part to think that religious beliefs had any bearing on dreams, but they were both of the Catholic faith, indeed the only two in the band and something lodged itself in my mind at the time. (I have never cared if a person's skin is black, white or a nice mixture somewhere between, which, I have no doubt, will be the ultimate outcome of integration as time goes by. The same goes for religion. As long as a person worships peacefully without causing trouble or prejudice, in the eyes of his personal deity, I have no desire to interfere. We are all "Jock Thampson's bairns" in the end anyway.)

However, I mustn't jump the gun! Or, indeed, let my personal feelings encroach on what I hope to be a fair recollection of a very important period in my life. I was enjoying every second of my existence. I had a career, money, girl-friends and a modicum of fame. At the age of twenty, what more could I ask? "Young Lochinvar" had indeed ridden out of the west (or in my case, the east) and was taking everything before him at a gallop.

There were, of course, little blips on what was generally a trouble-free horizon: like a request on "Two Way Family Favourites" for "Peter and the Wolf" by "Claude Valley and the Swingers"; or being told by a "last hope" fan after a particularly hard gig in Dumfries, "Excuse me Mr. Valley – but your band's 'duff'! (a Scottish euphemism for rubbish!) and probably, for me, the incessant necessity of playing banjo on ninety per cent of the band's repertoire. Trifles, but fond, funny memories worth recalling, I think.

My jazz musical appreciation was growing as quickly as my new-found frustration with the instrument which I found to be inhibiting in both its sound and the technique required to get any satisfaction from playing it. My personal jazz direction was definitely American-influenced with recordings of Louis Armstrong's Hot Five and All Stars, Jelly Roll Morton, Eddie Condon and the Benny Goodman Sextet, with the wonderfully inspirational genius, Charlie Christian. Forgive me for any delusions of grandeur, but they were untouchables to me, in contrast to my "Traddie" peers. The whole thing was made even worse by my discovery of Barney Kessel, Herb Ellis and Tal Farlow, who became personal gods and even superseded the hero of my teens, Django Reinhardt.

I am sorry for any suggestion of dissatisfaction on my part. I really was in the middle of a whole new exciting adventure, with glittering prizes awaiting me at its conclusion, if there ever was to be one.

Shangri La has a habit of not quite fulfilling one's euphoric idea of paradise. My particular version of the mystical wonderland proved to be no exception. As I approached the outskirts of the ultimate land, a few obstacles began to hinder my progress.

I had got over the death of my father and fulfilled my role as best man at Pete's marriage to Lori, been welcomed into the fraternity of the "banjo players' convention" and its followers and female collectors. Yes, my notch had been added to the guns of a couple of the more persistent – it's amazing how lovely tired old scrubbers appear after a few pints - but it was all given with a certain degree of shyness and hesitation. I discovered the talents of Italian hairdressers and tailors, in a purely professional way of course, I have already proclaimed my heterosexuality, and spent probably too much money on both but, what the hell, I was twenty years old and earning enough. Everything was going too well to anticipate any further set-backs, minor or otherwise.

Joe decided to have a party for some reason (I have a feeling it was Christmas time or New Year) at his Kilburn home. Irish cousins, would-be cousins, second cousins and cousins of cousins joined uncles, aunties, nephews and nieces, leprechauns and jazzers in a right old "hooley", if that's how you spell it. The Irish are wonderful "craic" hosts as you may have experienced from their wakes for one and general joie de vivre in life for the rest. Through all this, a nicely-rounded, heavily pregnant Mairead sat, queen like, sipping a glass of her family's wonderful brew, Guinness stout. Joe sang, jigged and scraped a fiddle at various times during the ceilidh and after enough black and gold had been accumulated, tried all three at the same time. If this was a party what happens at wakes?

It was, most unfortunately, not to last. How often is euphoria followed by its dark cousin, despair? Shortly after the party, Mairead went into labour and produced a baby girl, to the sheer delight of the band and, of course, Joe in particular, who had become a first time parent. At first, all was wonderful. Joe had taken a few days off to be with his new family, while we carried on with the gigs prior to, if my memory serves me well, (how I wish I had kept a diary!), setting off on a tour.

The telephone call that brought the desperate news that Joe's baby had a life-threatening blood disorder was an experience I hope never to revisit. The trumpet player was in a complete mess. This, of course, was 1962, long before the sophistication enjoyed in all walks of medicine and surgery today. A complete change of blood was necessary and even that had no guarantee of success. Joe decided it was probably best to leave the band. It was a devastating decision to everyone, but the correct one under the circumstances. We wished him all the best in the world and those of us who believed prayed, while the rest of us simply hoped. I can't remember who stepped in to take his place but I have a strong inkling it was Malcolm Higgins. Malky certainly did re-join, as history proves from recordings and films.

Joe's baby fortunately survived and a few months later the trumpeter joined the Terry Lightfoot organisation for a short period, before deciding to return to Northern Ireland to work in 'Showband' outfits, run by his cousin, Gay, who was a big success in the country of their birth. Sometime later, even more devastating news reached us, informing an incredulous, shocked band, of Joe's premature death of a heart attack. He was in his early thirties. Maybe dreams should be treated with more respect!

The next six, and last few, months of my involvement with the 'Clyde Valley Stompers' and Co. Ltd. don't give me as much pleasure in re-telling as the first six, but "all roads lead to Rome", as the saying goes and the story has to be told. Within a short period of weeks, Bert Murray, John McGuff, Robbie Winter and Bill Bain all left for pastures new or old. My memory, after fifty years or so without the aid of notes or diaries, does not serve me as accurately as I would like, but I don't think that any chronological accuracy/inaccuracy in their departure dates on my part either adds to or diminishes the facts as I recall them. They went, that is all that matters!

In Bert's case, it was a simple offer to join Alex Welsh's fine band and who can blame him for accepting an offer like that? Robbie was under pressure from a fiancée in Glasgow, in much the same way as Bill was given an ultimatum by his lonely wife in the same city. Likewise, a homesick John was, once again, itching to return to his family in Dalkeith. Replacing them was not to turn out to be as difficult as was expected. This time around, we knew who we wanted and there were plenty of applicants for the job.

For the first time, we had to deviate from the hundred percent Scottish ideal. Looking back, I think John must have been the first to be replaced, because his chair was taken, on Joe's recommendation by his friend from the Sid

Phillips Band, by Pete Hodge, who brought a new approach to the band, with his rounded Oxford accent and his ultra-correct technique. This last entry does not mean that he put technique before emotion. Far from it! He was and still is a hot Dixieland trombonist and an asset to any line up. It was just the strict demands of an ultra-precise Sid Phillips, who expected his sidemen to present a similar image. It's unfortunately too late to ask Kenny Ball of his experiences with the clarinettist, but I can tell you without fear of libel that he, Joe and Pete were all pleased to get away from the organisation. Pete brought a couple of amusing anecdotes with him, which brought a chuckle from the trombonist at the time they occurred, later from the "Clydes" in the telling and now I hope from you dear reader in the narration.

Sid's band was booked to play at a society ball in the Savoy. Although comfortable in this kind of gig, the band was reminded of the importance of their appearance and behaviour, especially in regard to alcohol. There was free champagne on offer, accepted in moderation by the majority of the chaps. Joe, it has to be said, wasn't a great drinker. By that, I don't mean he abstained, more that he couldn't hold it too well. In a nutshell, he had one glass of bubbly too many and, as he raised his trumpet to his lips, a small spray was emitted from his mouth.

"Get off the stand!",

yelled Maestro Sid. As he left towards the band room, which involved crossing the dance floor, mini-fountains of "champers" preceded him.

On another occasion, the drummer was, for some reason or another, left in charge of the "pads". This, I believe, took place in Park Lane so was, obviously, on another gig. At the end, after packing his drums and sorting out all the music, which obviously meant his leaving later than the rest, he started to silently fume. On reaching the street, his common sense departed him and he threw all the music books into the air. It was unfortunately quite a windy evening...............he arrived home even later than anticipated, after getting to know Park Lane quite intimately in his search for errant parts!

How do you replace a Malcolm Higgins or a Joe McIntyre? Kenny Ball, Bob Wallis and Alan Elsdon had their own bands. We had tried to replace Malky, unsuccessfully, with George Paterson, who had gone on to find success in a different direction. The search was on. The magnificent Kenny Baker had obliged on important recordings, but was obviously far too successful with his studio sessions.

We thought we had struck lucky with the availability of Glasgow-born, Alex Dalgleish, who had found himself discarded, firstly by Forrie Cairns and, later, by Terry Lightfoot, who had "inherited" Joe almost by default. He wasn't our answer either. Although Alex could certainly play and knew our repertoire, his personality was not quite right. Something just didn't fit! He was wrapped up in an engagement to a slightly domineering lady who, in the more important aspects of his life, was probably very good for him but, in the end, came between him and his future with the band.

Matters came to a head on a trip to the West Country. By this time, other personnel changes had hit the band and, although I can't remember the exact line up on the trip, I know Tony Baylis had replaced Bill Bain on double bass. We had left London in the morning and, by lunchtime, reached Taunton in Somerset and "Sheppey's Gold Medal Cider Farm". We pulled in on a whim and we were soon delighting in several samples, carefully administered by a gentleman in a green felt, flat cap perched atop a bright red countenance. A short-sleeved shirt revealed matching muscular arms and bright scarlet hands. His blood pressure was probably as high as the alcohol levels in his samples. There was, however, one vat that he wouldn't even countenance sharing. It took a fair bit of persuasion on our part to eventually coax a 'take- away of this obviously lethal brew from him and, even then, he would only let us have a mere half-gallon.

While all this was going on, Alex was silently fretting. A non-drinker or, at least, a minimal one by our standards, he had watched the time marching on and was getting more and more agitated with the thought of failing to be at Bristol Railway Station in time to meet a train his fiancée was travelling on. We eventually set off, but the trumpeter knew there was little hope of being at the station in time to meet her train. As we all cavorted, whooped and sipped the evil brew, he sat quietly in deep contemplation of his obvious impending berating. We were at least half an hour late, of course! We dropped him and drove off, arranging to meet at the gig later. I can imagine his reception to this day – a cowering, apologising figure, trying to explain the situation to an angry, umbrella- wielding lady unwilling to accept any excuse.

The gig itself was extremely interesting.

We were all well "in it" except, of course, Alex and banjo player Pat Wade, who was acting as our "roadie". As the set progressed, I felt more and more in need of a toilet break and was dreading having to stand up for any solo. Of course, that is exactly what happened! Pete called his featured number, "Oh Play to me Gypsy" which had half a chorus of banjo. I tried to warn him, but he insisted. I walked to the front of the stage for my solo and as I concentrated on playing, the floodgates opened. The legs of my heather-coloured band trousers turned dark with urine and my left shoe was suddenly soaking wet. I panicked and squished off the stage leaving a wet footprint as I exited. My last memories are of the faces of the disbelieving audience watching my disastrous departure. Fortunately, Pat was there to take over as I made my way back to the hotel, my race well and truly run. Next morning, I had the pleasure of ironing the sodden article of clothing dry enough to wear at an afternoon concert in Plymouth. On the way home to London that evening, Tony Baylis suddenly called out that he needed an emergency stop for a bowel movement. As he left the bus and headed for the bushes he was heard to say:

"Too late!"

Returning to the wagon sans discarded underwear he took his seat and we headed homewards. "Sheppey"'s cider had had the last laugh.

After a few weeks, Alex left and was replaced by a once again returning Malky Higgins. As I have already said, Bert Murray had also moved on to take up the offer from Alex Welsh which had always been on the pianist's wish list. His place was taken by Mick Mulligan star, Ronnie 'Bix' Duff, and the bassist was one, young Rognvald Mathewson, who had taken over from Tony. The former had first played trumpet in his native Aberdeenshire and the latter picked up the bass after a formal piano initiation into music in his native Lerwick, the main town in the Shetland Isles. The one hundred percent Scottishness of the band was once again ensured!

Chapter Nine

"Doctor, Doctor"

Once again we enjoyed a few months of settled personnel and musical stability. The rhythm section in my opinion had never been better. 'Bix' brought a different approach to the piano chair. Alex Shaw was a harmonic classic genius, while others in my early days had offered "stride" and "ragtime" as part of my education and Bert was completely, eccentrically, personal.

'Bix' had developed a more mainstream/modern liking through listening to people like Bobby Timmons and Joe Zavignol and built his solos from strong bass lines. His and those of young Ronnie were completely compatible, making it easy for me to find a chord pattern that fitted. The main problem was finding a drummer. Robbie Winter had gone and other London-based scots, such as the wonderfully enigmatic, Danny Craig, tried. Sandy Malcolm of the Royal Mile Jazz Band, mentioned in an earlier chapter, joined for a spell. The wonderful Len Hastings did some deps and even recorded a film track and a couple of singles with us, but he would rather have been German than Scottish. The drum chair was eventually filled by one of the best drummers I have ever known. Edinburgh-born Billy Law brought a new life to the band and a strong personal friendship was kindled between us.

This, as I have already stated, was, in my opinion, the best rhythm section the band ever enjoyed and it was probably one of the finest among the bands still riding the waves of the Trad Boom. To be truthful, we had stopped playing "Trad" months before, heading towards "Chicago Dixieland" and "Mainstream". I was spending more and more time listening to Charlie Christian and discovering the subtleties of Tal Farlow and Barney Kessel. The banjo was less and less featured in the band, as Pete headed toward the influences of Bennie Goodman and Artie Shaw. I remember playing a solo on the middle eight bars of "Memories of You" on Border Television. It sticks in my mind, as the producer's camera close-ups of my fingers on the strings required thick make-up to cover the natural sweat created by the warmth of the studio lighting. I wondered if it would hinder my playing, but I'm pleased to report that this was not the case and my performance proved satisfactory to all concerned.

This was also the most "fun" band of them all so far. The rhythm section was stable and swinging, the front line, with Malky back, musical and exciting. A similar sense of nonsense ran through the entire personnel - no "passengers", just good honest banter. If you want an example, I can tell you about a visit to the North Wales holiday resort of Rhyl. I can't recall anything about the gig but, in a Chinese restaurant afterwards, we created a face with a plate of noodles, two of Ronnie's prosthetic eyes, my upper denture and a tomato and called the waiter back………… Later, back in the hotel, it seemed like a good idea to Bix to see whether his theory that "This ham roll would taste better if you stuck it up your 'jeer' (Scottish for bum)," and proceeded to do as much, to the delight of an encouraging gallery. In actual fact, some of the pianist's unsavoury habits bordered on disgusting, but I will refrain from recounting them here and merely rely on any inquisitive reader with a strong constitution to ask me personally later. Another disgusting game was "lighting farts" in the wagon. When a suitable jet of methane was imminent from one of the chaps, we would make ready a naked flame from a match or lighter and hold it adjacent to the provider's trouser-clad anus and 'whoop' with glee at the resulting outcome. The more successful the result, the bigger the 'whoop'. Two occasions stick out in my memory. The first, recalled in the previous chapter, when after trying too hard, Tony Baylis, who was filling in between regular bassists, 'followed through' necessitating an immediate stop to again discard the soiled article of men's' apparel inadequately designed for the job. The second, more serious, was when Billy, sensing a 'real beauty coming on' decided to drop his trousers at the last moment. The aroma of singeing hair tells the rest of the story. Fortunately, there was no real damage done but the lesson was learnt

By then we had moved into a very nice house in a very nice part of very nice Finchley in a very nice part of North London. Unfortunately, the superlatives have to end at the end of the sentence. Would you believe that I can't even remember the name of the very nice street it was situated in? The extremely nice doctor who had welcomed us with a broad grin, rheumy eyes and a cigarette in his shaking hand, had a Northern

Irish accent, a very nice wife and an eccentric 'Kerry Blue' dog. I was to find out in a matter of weeks just who the eccentric in the trio was! The house spread over three floors, allowing separate single furnished rooms. Cooking and laundry and other menial tasks were 'down to us' but we could bring ladies home and stay up drinking all night if we liked. I should have spotted the obvious clue when I realised that Harry (the doctor) seemed to join us at all times of day or night, even clad in pyjamas. A strange masculine sort of lady had taken one of the other rooms, often appearing like an 'Addams Family' 'Morticia' as she descended the staircase to join in impromptu guitar-backed singalongs.

The curious became the obvious about a month after we moved in, when a removal van stopped outside and loaded up a good deal of the furniture and disappeared in the direction of Mill Hill and the M1 motorway, followed by a small car containing his wife and the eccentric dog. That's when things got really interesting!

Doctor Harry had, we discovered, spent many years in the Far East. Specialising in tropical and venereal diseases, he had decided enough was enough and had joined a practice in North London. Probably still in his fifties, though greying, he was a jolly, wiry sort of chap, with the Irish "gift of the gab" and a fondness for wine, women and song in that order. When he had married, I have no way of finding out, but I have a feeling his much younger, attractive wife was in the same line of business, so to speak. Maybe he talked his way into her life with his Celtic charm, but he couldn't talk her into staying after just a matter of months. He was alcoholic, obvious from our first meeting and a heavy smoker. Maybe his wife was prepared to accept the challenges these brought to their marriage, but I think the discovery of a third "body in the bed" was what "broke the camel's back". He didn't even attempt to hide 'Morticia', but I think expected her, on the contrary, to be welcomed with open arms, even though she was an "outed" Lesbian, with a partner of her own. I think Harry's Eastern experience had led him to believe "the more the merrier". A lot of this is personal speculation on my part but, looking back fifty odd years on, I believe more and more I was right. Anyway, as I have already stated, his wife left and the fun started.

The good doctor obviously had patients to administer to, a task he undertook in the style of that time, in surgery hours both in the morning and evening. This left his afternoons free for "boozing 'n' partying". A knock on your door and an invitation to join him in a wee drink announced his arrival home, although you often got pre-warning by his attempts to park his less-than-roadworthy VW 'Beatle'. The loss of necessary control over his pedal extremities was mostly the cause of the gear-crunching, scraping noises that were emitted from his efforts. How I wish I could produce a photograph of him! It would save all this word portrayal, but probably spoil the fun.

How we found this musician's paradise is lost in time, but I know that four of us moved in:

Ronnie Mathewson, who had replaced Bill Bain on bass, Sandy Malcolm, likewise on drums for Robbie and John McGuff, as well as yours truly.

The first to go was John. Sandy was next. Memory plays cruel tricks. Both Pete and I had remembered Sandy from the Royal Mile days in favourable light but, when it came to the crunch, he just didn't make it. Being a gentleman and a thoroughly nice one to boot, he actually recommended his successor, Billy Law. I personally have to say that, next to Lennie Hastings, Billy was one of the best drummers I have ever had the pleasure to play with. To this day, Scotland produces good drummers, for obvious reasons, but, with the exception of the late Murray Smith, Billy stood head and shoulders above most. So Billy moved "chez le Docteur", if you will excuse (with apologies and respect to Miles Kington) my "Franglais". The triumvirate of fun and frolics had ascended their thrones. The band continued to be popular and busy, which involved hundreds of miles of travelling weekly.

I seem to remember by this time having various road managers to pick us up, etc. Banjoist, Pat Wade, was certainly one of them and, in my fading memory, another was Sid Pye, a drummer augmenting his income by occasionally steering a bus for various bands. Sidney married a lovely lady called, I should think, Katherine. They naturally became affectionately known as Kate and Sydney Pye. (Think about it!) There were, of course, apart from the embryonic M1, no motorways, ensuring overcrowded trunk roads, such as the A5, A3, A1, etc. I have purposely named them in numerically reverse order because of the frequency we used them. They and their various watering holes and feeding stations became very familiar to us. We would leave our "digs at the Doc's", in the early morning, furnished with ample supplies of amnesiac lubrication such as "Merrydown" cider, etc., a quantity of which was immediately consumed on departure, in the desire to achieve a somnolent posture until the lunchtime watering hole was reached. These were usually of the "Tranny-Caff" variety such as "Jack's Hill" on the

A5 and "Chang's", I believe, on the A1. I believe it was the latter that offered:

"Egg and bacon and a cup of tea – 1/6. Plus, a sausage -1/9. Plus, beans – 2/- Plus toast -2/3. The Lot (all of this with mushrooms, black pudding etc.) –half a crown!"

There were also, of course, favourite pubs where, if time allowed, we enjoyed a game of darts. This was usually a game like "Shanghai" or another, I forget its name, which necessitated hitting designated segments of the board and adding up the successful "scores" – the one accumulating the largest total being the winner. The same pubs became favourites of all the bands, so it wasn't unusual to be joined by one off to a gig which required a similar route and travelling time, so the rivalry became more than musical, as budding "Jocky Wilsons" took on the equivalent "Eric Bristows."

After the gig and this, of course, was in the days before widespread fast food outlets and late-opening Chinese and Indian restaurants, the all night "Tranny" was a godsend to starving musicians who had foregone dinner in favour of a couple of pints in the nearest pub. A lot of clubs were unlicensed in the early 1960s, which led to stoking-up before and at the breaks in the performance and, of course, the mandatory "take-away" or "carry-oot". So the all-night "caff" became the equivalent of the desert oasis to the almost "nomadic" jazzers. I recall one on the way back from Ipswich, another on the journey from Bristol and a third, "The Ace" on London's 'North Circular' and fourth, "The Busy Bee", on the outskirts of Bushey, in Hertfordshire, respectively. The most used, however, was the "Blue Boar" at the northern extremity of the M1 motorway, which eventually almost became a meeting place for bands. It wouldn't be a surprise to find yourself sharing a table with compatriots from the Barber, Bilk, Lightfoot, Colyer or Elsdon bands, tired, hungry and slightly inebriated, next to one inhabited by

"H.A.L.D.S", our acronym of "hairy-arsed lorry drivers", scoffing huge meals, gulping endless mugs of tea or coffee or even sleeping on their forearms.

While we're talking of huge meals, I have to note that we had our champions in the likes of Robbie Winter, but the champion of champions has to be a bass player from another band who, out of respect, shall remain nameless. His usual "Bunter-like" midnight "snack" was

"Welsh Rarebit, chips, egg, bacon and beans twice please!"

I'll bet he snored and farted all the way home!

Back in the "wagon", we probably acted in a similar manner. As we drifted in and out of basically uncomfortable sleep, a nice little hangover would be developing, readying itself to do battle with what pianist Brian Lemon later referred to as a "Van Heusen" or "semi-stiff" (with acknowledgement of the famous shirt manufacturer.) Let me elucidate! When in the prime of life, a man's sexual awareness and indeed readiness, lies at the front of his brain. Do I really need to tell you that? Anyway tiredness and movement can trigger an embryonic erection at the most inopportune moment, creating contrasting feelings of discomfort and pleasure. As the blood rushes to accommodate appropriate parts of the body, the brain is engaged in a battle between torture and torment. A delicious banquet of pain and pleasure is presented to its suffering host. Fortunately, the weary traveller would be just too exhausted and hung-over to do anything about either and would just fall into bed exhausted.

The next morning, after a breakfast of painkillers and "Alka-Seltzer", we would be off again, neither willing nor ready to learn from our experiences, either then or now.

Chapter Ten

"Discontentment"

As gigs became more and more plentiful and widespread across the entire country, a couple of thoughts crept into our minds, mainly financial. Here we were, one night in Manchester, the next in Liverpool's famous "Cavern Club, followed by Chester, Birmingham, Coventry, a couple around London, Ipswich, Reading, Bristol and/or Cardiff. The reason for the choice of the latter two mentioned, is down to a Television programme which alternated weekly between the two cities. The programme was "Discs a Go-Go." Originally broadcast live under the title of "Cool for Cats" presented by the legendary band leader, Jack Jackson, ably assisted by Scottish singer, Glen Mason, it covered the "Hit Parade" of the 1960s. By the time we had entered the "charts" with "Peter and the Wolf", the show's name had changed, as had its presenter, who was none other than the famous wrestling authority, Canadian Kent Walton.

The band personnel had continually changed due to either homesickness, hatred of travelling or, in the case of a couple of guys, the wages. Don't get me wrong! We were paid as much as the musicians in any of the other bands and more than some of those in others, but the ratio between gigs and earnings in our case seemed questionable. As travelling minstrels, of course, our costs were also high, although there were perks to be had in the form of food and drinks supplied by managements or even fans. At this point in my life my culinary skills were restricted solely to the ability to cook the aforementioned omelettes but, in my defence, there were neither opportunities nor facilities to expand my expertise and, indeed, no requirement for either.

Things went on from day to day, week to week in much the same way. Billy befriended the niece of the great trumpet player, Al Fairweather. Pat was a lovely girl. She and Billy seemed to have a lot in common and their friendship developed. For me, the best thing about Pat, and I mean no disrespect to her in any way, was her friend, Janet Hughes. A bonnie girl with a glowing warmth, she entered my life in a big way. She came from Enfield in Middlesex, where she shared a home in, if I remember correctly, Willow Avenue, with her parents and brother, Roy. We became very close over the months we were together, even visiting Scotland on a couple of occasions. I even helped her parents by decorating their bathroom. At the time, I was a better paper hanger in my mind than in practice and I shudder to think what the finished job looked like. They thanked me anyway and it didn't seem to affect my relationship with their daughter. I really liked that girl! I do hope she married well and is still happy with whatever fate presented to her. While we went about our business learning new tunes, visiting new places, making new friends and generally accepting our "status quo", Pete was becoming more restless about his job as band leader, his relationship with "company directors", the attitude of the agency and the undemocratic way the money was dispensed and the non-transparency of 'royalties', radio, television and recording fees and such. He decided the time might be right to have a little chat with the powers that were!

As part of his responsibilities, he collected the money from the jazz clubs and occasional concerts, safely guarding it until "paying it in" at his regular meetings with either an agency representative such as Wally, a "floating" overseer who, like another, Colin Hogg, had had experience with the great Ted Heath Band, or on a visit to the office of the Lynn

Dutton Agency itself. It was on a fateful visit there, that he decided to put a brave face on things and let his feelings out. He very quietly and, in my opinion, courageously, put his points across and asked if it might be a suitable time to raise the band wages. Dutton listened to everything the clarinettist said and thanked him for his honesty, replying that he would consult the Directors of the Clyde Valley Stompers and Company, the main two being, of course, Ian Menzies and his wife. The very next day, Pete was called into the office to be informed of the Board's decision. He was to be dismissed as a troublemaker on the spot!

Called to the office to be informed of their decision, we,, to a man, without hesitation, decided that, if there was no Pete, there was no band. We resigned and walked out of the office.

About a week later, the last line-up of the Clyde Valley Stompers functioning in these islands was formed. It might have worked but for, in my opinion, two things. The first was the rise of the "Beatles" and the "Mersey Sound." The second and much more important reason for failure was the inescapable fact that, with the exception of the bass player, not one of the new band was Scottish! An already formed British band, 'The Leather Town Jazz Band' were plying their trade somewhat unsuccessfully in Germany. They answered the Company's call to become 'Clyde Valley Stompers'. Greed had overcome democracy and common sense yet again.

Any fleeting admiration or respect I had for Ian Menzies and his money-at-all-costs principles disappeared that day. In all walks of jazz life, you will encounter musicians you find inspiring, yet blasé, encouraging, yet lacking in sympathy, amusing, yet sad and even lovable, yet cold. The music creates friendship, respect, admiration and acceptance. It is a brotherhood, a comradeship, a camaraderie, a club. The membership is for life. Menzies didn't fit in anywhere, in my humble opinion. He treated equals and, in most cases, musical superiors, as servants in his quest to fill his coffers. As I write this, my animosity grows. Better left alone!

-

Chapter Eleven

"Brussels Sprouts to Haggis"

It wasn't just the "Clydes" who were in trouble, however – the whole "Trad" bubble was about to burst. One by one "jazz" promoters deserted the sinking ship to cling on to the life rafts of the embryonic strains of "Rhythm and Blues".

Pete, with the encouragement of his newly- redundant cohorts, decided to stick around to see what happened. Borrowing the name from the inspirational, legendary Louis Armstrong and, still clinging to a Caledonian theme, he inserted the word "Scottish" into the mix and "Pete Kerr's Scottish All Stars" were formed. A phoenix rising from the dying embers of the smouldering, spluttering remnants of a once healthy bonfire. The band was comprised of most of the line-up that had "walked the plank" off the sinking ship. The crew list read as follows: Pete Kerr on clarinet; Mike Scott, a young Devonian, on trumpet; Eddie Lorkin, newly-graduated from the Glasgow School of Music, on trombone; Jim Douglas, who owned both a guitar and a banjo; Londoner, Mike Oliver, on piano; Ron Mathewson on double bass and Billy Law at the drums.   Both Mikes were "honorary" Scots, whereas Eddie, being a Glaswegian, was 'nearly acceptable' and, in later years, made a good reputation for himself with the BBC Radio Orchestra.

Our first obstacle was where to live. Without a regular source of gigs (in truth, nothing in the diary at all) there was no income. Some of the wiser among us had saved a "few bob" but most of us had lived the "life of Reilly", spending what we earned in the belief that it would never end. I was in the latter group, of course! A couple of the chaps, having had regular jobs, were eligible for the "Dole". Another came from a well-to-do family, who agreed to subsidize his income and Pete had taken a rented property in East Finchley, which he shared with his wife, Lori and recently born son.

In truth, it was a relief to leave the "Doc's". He had become more and more demanding of our free time, at the same time drinking more than his practice was prepared to accept. Like us, he was on a parallel downward spiral. I think, in the end, he lost the house and, eventually, was forced to live a mediocre existence as a locum. I was really sorry this part of my life was closing in on me. I had really enjoyed my time there and his happy but desperate approach to life was quite influential in a small way. Good on you, Doc! I do hope things worked out for you!

Through someone knowing someone who knew someone in the band, we somehow acquired the tenancy of a house in upper-market, Chandos Road, in East Finchley. Pete gave up his rented flat, settling his family with his parents back in Haddington. We moved in *en masse*, taking over the entire property. Who in their right mind would let six testosterone-filled, under-financed, musically-frustrated, under-nourished young men loose in his or her home? Someone did!

I don't remember much about how we existed – probably better that I don't – but I do remember free vegetables, especially sprouts, from a kind lady next door and the odd trip "up west" when the dole money came in. There were rows, of course, which eventually culminated in our eviction. Two, in particular, are etched in my memory. The first was a personal fight between the trumpet player and me over a minute personal matter blown out of all proportion by the tensions of our existence. The skirmish resulted in bruises and a swollen lip for the trumpet player, who might, in other circumstances, have been dependent on the latter and swollen knuckles for myself, equally protective of that part of my anatomy on which my livelihood had depended.

The second, much more serious incident, brought the whole thing to a head. An argument had sprung up between Eddie and Billy, the trombonist and drummer respectively. It became heated. Snarling faces and raised arms emitted harsh words and tentative blows. The combatants repaired to the kitchen, where the volume of the shouting escalated. Suddenly, the drummer burst into the living room with a look of horror on his face, locking the door between them. There was a serving-hatch between the two rooms which had obviously not been built to accommodate what was now coming through its moderate aperture – a crimson-faced trombonist, shouting murderous obscenities and brandishing a dangerous-looking kitchen knife.

Peace was, of course, restored but the

writing was on the wall. We were up against it musically, with the rise in popularity of the "Beatles" in particular and "Rhythm and Blues" in general. We were up against it financially and we were up against it in our personal relationships. "Scottish All Stars" or "Clyde Valley Has-beens"? It was time for a re-think, a change of environment, a radical metamorphosis and the only place for all this to take place was back in Edinburgh. Back to square one again – too many snakes – not enough ladders

Chapter Twelve

"Edinburgh Rocks"

If any of you ever doubted or indeed have never experienced a mother's love and patience, I dedicate this chapter to one abounding with both.

Never mind the facts already chronicled, such as her struggle to bring up a family of five, look after a partially-sighted mother and a recently demobilised brother virtually single-handed, the financial sacrifices she made to please her children, which included the obvious hardship in buying my first guitar, her acceptance in letting me 'flee the nest' for pastures anew in Germany and her willingness to let me disappear yet again southward to 'make my fortune', are all examples of her patience, unselfish love and understanding.

Now here we were - six out-of-work musicians and one wife - descending on her home, testing her hospitality beyond any form of normality and expecting her to greet us with open arms!

"Come away in, boys and lassie, welcome tae ma hoose and make yersels at hame. Ye'll be hungry! Granny's made a pot o' soup, tae warm ye up!"

Her words, welcoming and warm, relaxed the chaps. The three-bedroomed, semi-detached council house at Number Three, Park Crescent, Gifford, now slightly bulging at the walls, was somehow expected to accommodate us in addition to its usual incumbents, for a few days until other 'digs' were found. Days turned into weeks and (in a some cases) weeks into months. I still don't know how, but she found beds for all of us, fed and watered us, listened to our petty problems, handled our unruly drunkenness and calmed the troubled waters when little storms broke out. She became the not-so-old 'lady who lived in a shoe' except that somehow she did know what to do. She was actually 'in her element!'

Mother Earth ruling majestically! Granny cooked and washed and, with the beneficial, occasional help of little glasses of her home-made elderberry wine, often disappeared into nostalgic memories of better times and occasionally played her fiddle, which she cossetted comfortably under her ample left breast. She would scrape away at obscure Scottish and Irish melodies, slightly toneless and a little out of tune, with the vigour of a Menuhin or Grappelli, but with, alas, none of their dexterity.

For a couple of weeks, we lived as one big family. One by one the chaps, in looking for privacy and independence, found other accommodation. Pete, of course, was at home in Haddington, as was Billy in Edinburgh. Mike 'O' and his wife found a furnished room nearby and Mike 'S' and Eddie similar digs in Edinburgh. Ronnie stayed longest. He undertook a mild flirtation with my sister, much to the annoyance of her future husband, Ronnie, who bided his time with grace and dignity. We rehearsed endlessly in various pubs and rooms in Edinburgh, managing to acquire a few local gigs in venues such as 'The Place' in the Grassmarket area of the city and some not-so-local, such as Thurso in the north and Hawick in the south. We even spent an interesting week in Lerwick, the main town in the Shetland Isles and home of the 'Musical Mathewsons'. A local chemist, 'Spew' Campbell, who liked a glass or two and a grocer called 'Drew', who had the biggest collection off vinyl jazz records I have ever seen, welcomed us with open arms to their jazz-starved town. The week was not without its moments, musical and otherwise. Most, naturally, were alcohol- fuelled, including the desire at dawn one day near the end of the visit when some of us, finding a box of kippered herrings in the harbour, (no, I don't know how they got there!) decided they would be happier back in the sea and undertook their repatriation by flinging them into the oily water. We were lucky to get away with that one!

It seemed like a good idea to record a couple of our better arrangements. Returning to the same studios we had used five years previously, the band produced two extended play, seven inch discs on the 'Waverley' label. It would be nice to listen to them again – I must have copies somewhere.

Billy Law, Ron's Mum, Mike Scott, Ron Mathews, Ron"s Dad, Pete Kerr, Eddie Lorkin, Mike Oliver and Jim Douglas .Lerwick Harbour, Shetland 1963

INTERMEZZO

"Foreword to the Past!"

It was, of course, almost impossible to include every musician or venue ever played with or at, in the eighteen years or so of my involvement with the great Alex Welsh Band, in my book, "Tunes, Tours and Travelitis" which has enjoyed and indeed is still enjoying successful sales and reviews. At least a couple of musicians and one promoter have expressed a little disappointment at not being mentioned considering their substantial contributions to the history of the band. As a forerunner to this my second effort, I am endeavouring to put that right by digging deep into a somewhat less but nevertheless adequate pool of memories to provide suitable information on the subject which, of course, must involve "Travelitis." I will start in a chronological order with the musicians, instrument by instrument with suitable anecdotes 'thrown in' for good measure. It might be pertinent to include regular deputies who became band favourites during my time. Let me start in the engine room with the

DRUMMERS:

Len Hastings and Roger Nobes, are both well represented in "T, T and T." Between their respective years several were tried but for one reason or another, with all due respect to their talent and ability they didn't quite match up to what Alex was looking for. Included, among others who have slipped out of my memory cells, were the late Tony Allen and Graham Scriven and Billy Law who is still with us but unfortunately not playing. Ron McKay was approached but refused on the misguided self-belief that he couldn't fill Len's shoes. After Roger's departure, the band was entering its final years and the drum chair was filled, on what gigs there were, by Martin Guy and finally Laurie Chescoe who suited Alex's return to his beloved "Dixieland." Looking and listening in a backward direction has been made easier with the discovery and digital re-mastering of tapes of the band in what I believe to be their finest hours. To me Len Hasting stands head and shoulders above any 'pretenders' to his throne.

BASSISTS:

Bill Reid left shortly after my arrival in the band to be replaced by the enigmatic Shetlander, Ron Mathewson. He in turn vacated his place on the podium to fellow Scot, Ronnie Rae. This succession was to be repeated once more before Harvey Weston brought a regular line-up to the rhythm section. During this trio's short reigns as kings of the lower register, Tony Baylis, who brought his sousaphone to the ensemble and travelled to Newport, Gerry Higgins, two Brian Jones's and a young Dave Holland all came and went. On Harvey's departure a new sound was introduced by Pete Skivington on bass guitar. At first frowned upon by purists and questioned by Alex himself, his good sense of time and the fact that he is probably the only bass guitarist able to produce the sound the a more authentic viol.

After his departure, tradition was restored by the engagement of Len Thwaites and Ron Rubin.

PIANISTS:

When Brian Lemon left, the band entered a period of trial. How do you find a replacement for two of the best, although quite radically different in style, jazz pianists this country has ever produced? Several come to the foreground of my memory. The late Brian Leake filled in for some gigs although still a member of Alan Elsdon's fine band. I considered him to be a bit of an enigma. Well educated, with a good grasp of the English language which he pronounced with a university style delivery he was totally left wing in his politics. Nothing wrong in that, I hear you ask! He resided in a large house in a good part of Richmond on Thames which was well furnished and might be considered in the upper middle class bracket. He was also an active trade unionist and was the local secretary of the M U.   Was he a "right wing Socialist" or "left wing Conservative"? I don't know, is the answer and probably he was the only one who did!   He adopted a slight air of superiority which was often displayed   when ordering food:

To an Indian waiter –

"Do you have halibut?"

"Yes Sir!"

"Bring me a Halibut Phal, then!"

The bogg mindles!

Colin "Barney" Bates joined for a while. He was with the band in 1979 at the Nice Festival when the news of Lennie's death reached us. I liked Barney very much both as a man and a pianist but his time with Alex was limited. Before joining he had become besotted with a French co-presenter of "Three, Two, One" a television quiz programme. Unfortunately, he was getting financially over his head in hopelessly wooing her. On one occasion in Lubeck, he kept the whole band waiting in the bus while he was on the phone to her in London, rushing out of the kiosk at one stage to ask Alex for some more Deutschmarks and scurrying back to insert them in the machine.

"*What was all that about?*"

Alex asked him on his entering the bus.

"*An argument about the size of the Electricity Bill*"

Was his reply! Barney has a wicked, dry sense of humour as well as a talent as an artist and a fine ability to play jazz piano. It was he who on a night off on in West Germany on a trip to the Dresden Festival, told us the wonderful story, which you may or may not have heard, about two famous actors who didn't mind a drink or ten, Robert Newton and Donald Wolfitt who, while in a period play, had partaken of a drop or two before curtain up. Accused by a member of the audience,

"*Sir, you're drunk!*"

Newton replied:

"If you think I'm drunk, wait till you see the Duke of Buckingham!"

Wonderful! Barney left to be replaced by various other fine players including Ron Rubin who handled the horizontal eighty-eight keys with equal dexterity to the more upright double bass. Another Collin Bates, in this instance Australian and sporting two 'Ls' in his first name came and went between accompanying George Melly and returning to the Antipodes.

GUITARISTS:

On the few occasions I missed gigs through illness or some other reason, John

Attwood, a young Martin Taylor and later Dave Cliff, Paul Sealey and Denny Wright filled in for me. Alex knew how to pick a guitar player!

FRONT LINE:

Deputies were few. Alan Cooper, Danny Moss, and mostly Al Gay on saxophones and Jim Shepherd and later George Howden on trombone deserves a chapter in his own right. I intend including one as this book unfolds and you will read how our musical paths often crossed.

TRUMPET:

There were few trumpet players in the time of Alex's existence who could lead an ensemble like him. Alan Elsdon nearly succeeded. Ray Crane made up for his lack of drive with lyrical musicality and an up and coming Digby Fairweather brought a new direction. Others like Gerry Salisbury, Pat Halcox and Dickie Hawdon were a delight. The best was of course Kenny Baker who could grace any band or orchestra in the universe but was difficult to book because of his involvement in television studio work. In my opinion not one of those could drive a band like Alex did.

So there you have it! If I have missed you out again, a thousand apologies.

Please let me know and I'll get the pen and paper out again for a third and probably final attempt to make it up to you.

"Herr" Lennie 'sitting in' at the Zillertal, Hamburg.
We had to fork out for a round of drinks which did not
please Alex too greatly but he did manage a smile for the
photo! "Ein Prosit!"

Jim Douglas

PART TWO

Roger Nobes, 'The Invisable Man' and Brian
Lemon on the way to Scapa Flow

"Travelitis"

Chapter Thirteen

"'Fallout' Road"

When Billy Law and I arrived back in London, we had to find somewhere to stay, of course. I think it was Billy who found the room and kitchen in Alexandra Park Road, Muswell Hill that I described in the opening of my first book, "Tunes. Tours and Travelitis". It was at the end of Autumn / beginning of Winter, 1963. The room was cold and sparsely furnished, heated by one of those bottle gas heaters and with almost nowhere to store or hang clothes. The kitchen was adequate – nothing more.

To pay my share of the rent I was hired to work for our Greek landlord in his shoe manufacturing factory in Old Street, EC. Every morning I caught a bus there, sat down at a table stacked high with parts of ladies' shoes, which I was required to stick together with a latex-based adhesive. I worked in my own silence for a designated number of hours, five days a week. I say silence, but I am probably misleading you by using the word to describe the lack of English conversation. What conversation there was came in a babble of Greek across the background of clattering, professional sewing machines. My own brain was constantly filled with one thought:

"What the fuck am I doing here?"

Billy started to get a few gigs, leaving me to my own boring company more and more. I really nearly packed it all in but, somehow, soldiered on until that fateful Sunday night at the "Fishmonger's Arms" in Wood Green, when I "sat in" with the Alex Welsh Band.

Within a short space of time, probably a few weeks at most, we were able to leave our frozen prison. I packed in my job, told the landlord we were going and moved into separate rooms that had become available at the famous house in Fawley Road, West Hampstead. The house was completely rented by jazz musicians. At the top was bassist Tony Baylis and his girlfriend, Heather. Next door to him, the original incumbent, Peter Nixon, a solicitor by profession, had returned to his native North East, leaving his vacant room for Billy to move into. On the first floor, the room opposite the one I was to move into, was occupied by saxophonist Ned Thompson and his wife, Judy. My room had been tenanted by the wonderful pianist, Colin Purbrook, who had also found pastures new. At ground level were situated two larger rooms occupied by two grand pianos and two equally grand pianists, Keith Ingham and his French wife and the wonderful Brian Lemon. The basement boasted a kitchen hardly used, but for the brewing of tea and coffee and the consumption of the occasional bowl of "Cornflakes" and the likes. Perhaps the women did cook a little, but I was never up early enough to catch them. Lunch was usually of the liquid variety in one of the nearby pubs and dinner, if you were at home and not gigging somewhere, served at the Indian restaurant at the end of the road across West End Lane. All day long the sound of practice, interrupted by an occasional fit of coughing by Brian, the result of the inhalation of too many cigarettes, came from the piano rooms. I found this quite inspiring and it led to the only period of my musical career in which I undertook any serious "woodshedding" of my own.

I was doing all of Alex's engagements by now. I had first heard the band live in Edinburgh's Prince's Street Gardens when I was about eighteen or so. I have to admit to not being overly enthusiastic with what I heard, apart from John Richardson's drumming, which I thought 'amazing'. Naively, I thought our band to be better!

Listening to the famous recordings of that band with Archie, Roy Crimmins, Fred Hunt, Chris Staunton and "J R", now, I realise how wrong I was! On the next occasion I came across them, it was as an equal, after I had just joined the "Clydes" at an "All-nighter" in Birmingham Town Hall. By this time, Lennie Hastings had replaced John Richardson, bringing his eccentricity with him and Tony Pitt was adding his potent voice on banjo and guitar. I was most impressed by the latter.

Extraordinary as it may now sound, after the initial success of the Beatles and the subsequent decline in "Trad", Tony and I sincerely thought about forming a similar group with Tony's brother Vic on bass and a drummer yet to be selected. The plan was soon shelved after we realised that none of us were singers! Soon after, Tony left Alex to join Kenny Ball's Band.

I was offered my first couple of gigs with Alex at this period before joining the band. Archie was still just about well enough to play, but Al Gay, who had left the Bob Wallis Band, stood by and joined the front line, much in the same way he did when John Barnes was injured in the now famous road accident. Although Alex didn't seem to have any recollection of this, I can assure you I was there and enjoyed it enormously.

In the early days after "joining", I mean before hearing the magic words from the leader that I was now a *bona fide* member, Alex had formed a "Big Band" for several engagements. I was lucky enough to occupy the "Freddy Greene" chair on two occasions. The line-up was: Roy Crimmins, Tony Milliner and George Chisholm on trombones; Alex, Kenny Baker, Tommy McQuater and Bobby Pratt, trumpets; Archie Semple, Al Gay, Red Price and Ronnie Ross, reeds; Bert Murray on piano; Bill Reid, bass; Len Hastings drums and a spotty-faced, runny-nosed "Herbert" on guitar. At this time, my soloing was sparse but not non-existent. Gradually I got a few more solos on which I tried to emulate Tony. At the interval on one gig, Alex approached me at the bar:

"Fancy a taste?"

he asked.   On my accepting his offer he continued;

"Why do you try to be Tony Pitt? I hired you because you're the best rhythm guitar player around and, what's more, I think you could be a good soloist in your own right."

The words stuck! Thanks Alex.

Jim Douglas

After Archie's declining health forced him to leave, Al agreed to step in until a replacement was found. He was wonderful to play with and great company to boot. On a journey to Exeter, just the two of us in his own car, to fulfil the second of the Big Band gigs mentioned, I learned an awful lot about this great player, his history and aspirations, likes and dislikes and his tastes in music. Our paths were to cross numerous times in the course of the next twenty years or so. In all that time I never heard him play in any way but wonderfully. He was the consummate master of his craft. With your indulgence, I would like to insert an obituary I wrote for him in a North East Jazz publication. I wrote:

"Al was born in London on 25th February, 1928. He began to play the clarinet in his teens and studied at the Guildhall School of Music and first played in his brother Joshua's band after which he went on to lead his own in 1944. In 1946 he joined a band which rejoiced in the

name of the "Jive Bombers." After Conscription, another form of National Service followed in the shape of "Geraldo's Navy" working in bands on the famous Cunard liners.

Back on terra firma, his first big professional break came in April 1955 when he joined the Freddy Randall band. The Randall band was a breeding ground for talent with people like Bruce Turner, Archie Semple, Lennie Felix, Brian Lemon, Lennie Hastings, Dave Shepherd and Roy Crimmins passing through its ranks. Al had a break from Randall during which he had a short spell with a Bobby Mickleburgh outfit, but re-joined Randall six months later.

Al made his first recordings with Freddy's band. But the latter's commercial timing was terrible; he disbanded in February 1958, just before the lucrative "Trad" Boom peaked and didn't reform until 1963 when it was effectively over. Al then joined the Gold Brothers' Pieces of Eight until 1960,, when he had a year's spell with drummer Joe Daniels' band. In early '61 he led his own quartet on board the Queen Mary. In May of that year he joined Bob Wallis, who had been seeking a player able to play several reed instruments at a high standard. Al had been playing tenor and soprano for a while, but his previous bands had also sported sax players and he had been mainly confined to clarinet. However, this oversight was soon corrected, as can be heard on the 1962 "Wallis Collection" album where Al steals the show on all three instruments. (At one stage the line-up included the Humphrey Lyttelton rhythm section of the previous year which consisted of Ian Armit, piano, Pete Blannin, bass and Eddie Taylor on the drums). In November of 1964, a break-away group called Blues by Six was formed, which included Al. This proving unsuccessful, he joined "Long John" Baldry and the "Hoochie Coochie Men" until they disbanded in July 1965. (A young Rod Stewart used to carry his instruments for him!) Al then gigged around London during 65/66 playing again with Bob Wallis, Freddy Randall, trumpeter Colin Smith, the London City Stompers and Ian Armit's house *band at the Georgian Club. He also did a lot of BBC radio work with his own quartet including his old Randall colleagues Brian Lemon and Stan Bourke. During this period Al also played with the Australian folk group, "The Seekers."*

Bad luck gave Al a lucky break in January 1967. The Welsh band's reed player John Barnes had been badly injured in a road crash involving the band coach. Al got the job "temping" for him. However, in the best traditions of good jazz bands when John returned, Al stayed on to help John's convalescence. On the gigs where both brought all their instruments, the stage positively groaned. Ralph Laing recalls that on one occasion, when both guys fielded a quintet, a local newspaper billed it as the "All gay Joan Barnes Quintet".

Al left Alex in late 1970 and spent a quiet spell during which he played gigs with bassist Ron Russell and also in 1974, again with Freddy Randall. From 1975 he played with Lennie

Hastings's band and Stan Greig's London Jazz Big Band (until '83). In 1977 he played and recorded with trombonist Charlie Galbraith and yet again for his old employer, Freddy Randall.

In September of the same year Al received a call again from Alex who was replacing John Barnes after thirteen years. This third and last spell lasted, with a year's break for Alex's illness, until the latter's untimely death in June 1982. During this period Al also deputised with the World's Greatest Jazz Band of Bob Haggart and Yank Lawson and in 1978, with the Harlem Jazz & Blues Band on the Continent. He also toured with trumpeter Harry Edison in 1980.

After the break-up of the Welsh band, Al joined forces with trumpeter Keith Smith and eventually joined him from September 1990 to February 1992 to undertake a tribute tour to celebrate the centenary of Cole Porter featuring Paul Jones, Elaine Delmar and a rhythm section of pianist Mick Pyne, guitarist Jim Douglas, bassist Harvey Weston and drummer Bobby

Worth. From 1986 to 1997 Al played extensively with Digby Fairweather in the latter's Val Wiseman-Billie Holiday presentations "Lady Sings the Blues, his "Jazz Super Kings" and the "First Class Sounds" aggregations for the Post Office and which also featured Jim Douglas in all three. He was also included in various versions of the Welsh Reunion bands and also played with U.S. visitors Peanuts Hucko and Red Norvo.

In December 1998 the ailing Dave Jones left drummer Laurie Chescoe's Good Time Band and sadly died shortly after. Laurie brought in Al who played with the band until November of 2002 when he decided to give up touring. After a short retirement with his second wife, Al developed Alzheimer's and passed away in a care home in Dunstable in December 2013.

After several weeks with the band, bassist Bill Reid decided to quit and young Ronnie Mathewson joined. Most of the history of what happened to the band from then on is chronicled in my previous publication so, with your kind indulgence and in the hope that those of you who are unfamiliar with it may be encouraged to acquire a copy, I will resume my tale in a more personal manner.

Chapter Fourteen

"Stanwick Road, W14"

Ron Mathewson was already in London when he got the call to join the band. He had been part of an outfit organized by drummer 'Fat John' Cox to fulfil some gigs in Germany. Whether or not he had permanent digs in the Earls Court / West Kensington area, or was staying with the Coxes, I can't remember. I do know, however, that that is where he found a two room maisonette in a street off North End Road, which we agreed to share. Alex lived not far away in Pennant Mews, W8 and it seemed that, with none of the three of us able to drive, it would be beneficial if we could be reasonably close at hand for pick-ups etc. Ron had officially joined in the April of 1964 and I believe we moved in a few weeks later.

That's when the fun really started! But not at first!

One of the first gigs we did together was at a jazz club in Maidstone in Kent. During the course of the evening my eye was drawn to the pub ashtrays on the tables and I thought how nice one would look on our coffee table in the living room of our flat. At the end of the performance while waiting for Len to pack his drums I asked the landlord if he would consider selling me one.

"Take one of those on the table, with the Brewery's compliments!"

He offered.

After being dropped off in North End Road, we had just turned into Stanwick Road when a police car drew up. Two officers jumped out:

"Where did you get that instrument and what are you concealing under your jacket?"

I had tucked the ashtray inside the bottom of my jacket to purposely disguise what it was, but I suppose it did look a bit suspicious. When I explained where I had acquired it, one of the young "Bobbies" said:

"Oh yes? Pull the other one mate!

Without further ado I was bundled into the

car and whisked off to make a statement at Hammersmith Police Station. I was just filling in the details when the duty Sergeant came in:

"Jim? Jim Douglas? Is that you?"

He asked. Would you believe this? It turned out to be a chap I had been to school with! On hearing my "defense" he, without a word, got the telephone number of the pub, woke up the landlord who confirmed my story and arranged forthwith to get a car to take me back to Stanwick Road. The curious thing is that, although we promised to meet up under better circumstances and share a pint, I never saw him again.

Our rooms, on the top floor of the Edwardian terraced house in Stanwick Road, London W14, was perfectly situated for us with its proximity to the A4 Cromwell Road and West Kensington Underground station, a mere half dozen stops from Piccadilly and one from the centre of "Kangaroo Valley", Earl's Court. The area was a single man's dream-come-true in the "Swinging Sixties" as the decade became known. Pubs, restaurants, flats full of single, party-minded girls, "The Beatles," the "Stones," Carnaby Street – an age of sexual freedom and fun – it was definitely the place to be. (Conversely, although the availability of the contraceptive pill had eased the burden of unwanted pregnancy, it opened a real can of worms which crawled and wriggled their ways into the essence of old-fashioned morality and set the seeds of a lack of responsibility from which we have never recovered.)

Ron and I joined in the frivolous fiasco with free abandon. We had two New Zealand girls sharing the flat below us, a quiet couple on the ground floor and in the basement, a trio of Australian "Sheilas" who included the lovely Judith Durham, the sweet voiced singer of the "Seekers."

So there was of course, wine, women and

song - all served up with the bravado of youth in abundance, in a background of comfort and security. The flat was indeed comfortable, clean, modern and spacious. What had been two good-sized rooms at the top of the stairs had been tastefully transformed into a well-decorated, beautifully furnished, well-appointed "palace", far too good for a couple of young Scottish reprobate jazz musicians with probably one thing on their minds apart from finding somewhere to hang their hats and lay down their weary frames. Bearing in mind that Ron was still finishing his "Sexual Awareness Apprenticeship", the signs were that he was going to graduate with flying colours, while I was happy to settle with the moderate qualifications I had earned, which brought their own rewards, without the frantic need of personal proof that I had earned them.

But this a reminiscence of times learning my trade as a musician and I must try to stick to this. You, dear reader, must be the judge of whether or not I venture too far from this task but I feel that, in your interest, you might appreciate an anecdote or two etched in my memory and which might raise a chuckle from the less "expeditious" of you.

I mentioned that Ron had joined in the April, which meant we were obviously in the flat by the summer months. This is substantiated by the memory of the two of us going on swimming trips to the "Serpentine" lake in Hyde Park. Although the water was never exactly warm, we enjoyed our "dips", even to the extent of befriending a couple of old chaps who ensured us they never missed a daily swim, three hundred and sixty-four days a year, in all weathers and temperatures. Getting to Hyde Park involved a short trip on the Underground railway and a medium walk through the streets of Kensington. There were clothes lockers available at a price at the facility but, like many others, we discreetly changed with the aid of a towel by the lake-side, leaving our clothes in a neat pile within eye-sight. Ron was fastidious about his apparel, always making sure his neatly-pressed trousers were folded "just-so" and the rest of his clothes piled carefully on top of them. One day, we came out of the water to find that his shirt and trousers were missing. My crumpled heap of clothes was as I had left it. Of course, no one had seen a thing. Walking back to West Kensington and riding the "Tube" was quite interesting. I often wonder what passers-by made of a red-faced, embarrassed young man and his plainly caring, but not-really-wanting-to-know partner-in-crime and what they were up to. Mind you, it was the enlightened years of the early "sixties", so maybe "anything goes" was the acceptable answer.

So, for the first time in a couple of years I felt that my career was back on track. I was comfortably housed, employed, young, ambitious and happy. Although the band wages were less than we had enjoyed with the "Clydes", with careful husbandry we just about "got by". We even managed to host the odd party or twelve.

With the return of Fred Hunt and the addition of one of best bassists I ever worked alongside, together with arguably the best drummer around, the rhythm section seemed to settle down. The frontline of Alex, Roy Crimmins and Al Gay put the icing on the cake. The Band was still struggling a little bit in the tidal wave created by the "tsunami" of the Rhythm and Blues upsurge of course, but there were enough "die hard" clubs around the length and breadth of the country, to eke out an existence. In no geographical order of preference, we visited Carlisle and the "Pheasant Inn", drove along close to Hadrian's Wall to appear in Newcastle-upon-Tyne, headed south to Teesside and the Coatham Hotel in Redcar, staying up all night at the "Zetland" Hotel, before setting off, hung-over and tired next morning, to travel to Leeds or Sheffield or Rotherham or Nottingham or Derby. Or we might travel up the newly-built M1 Motorway to perform at Leicester, Coventry, Birmingham or Trentham Gardens near Newcastle under Lyme, with the final destination of Manchester or Liverpool at the end of the rainbow. This reads as if we were undertaking well-planned tours. Sometimes we did, but it was generally, more often, the opposite situation! Because clubs often held their sessions on the same nights, one-night-stands, in the original meaning of the words, were very often necessary. Without today's road structure, journeys were long and arduous – hour upon hour of sitting behind slow-moving trucks and lorries on 'A' and 'B' grade roads, with only the dubious refreshment stops at "Greasy Spoon" transport cafes or mind-numbing alcohol top-ups at "the next pub we see, Chaps" to look forward to.

East of London, the A12 took you through Essex and into Suffolk. Essex boasted Colchester Jazz club, a Sunday evening venue still going strong while, in the latter, the "Ronanda" organization had a club in Ipswich. They also promoted the popular Manor House gig in north east London. In the South, Brighton hosted the most extrovert one of all. Run by a promoter by the name of Bonnie Manzi, I believe of Italian, Jewish origin, the Aquarium Function Suite enjoyed regular crowds attending the "Chinese Jazz Club" – "Vellee Good Hot Jazz". He also ran a successful club in Bristol without the Oriental influence.

In the Home Counties and Greater London, itself, clubs were many, from the "George" in Morden, the "Whittington" in Pinner, the Rugby Club, Osterley Park, gigs in St Albans, Luton, Uxbridge, Golders Green, the "Thames Hotel" at Hampton Court and, of course, the "Fishmongers Arms" in Wood Green and the "100 Club" then known as "Jazz Shows Jazz Club". There were obviously enough gigs to go around. One by one, they were deserting the sinking "Good Ship Trad".

It was in the Autumn of that year that a minor miracle happened for the Band. A young jazz enthusiast in Manchester, Jack Swinnerton by name, had dreamed of maybe one day hearing some of his idols in the flesh. There had been notable visitors to these shores stretching back to the Original Dixieland Jazz Band, Louis Armstrong and Eddie Condon in the 1950s and solo appearances by George Lewis and Django

Reinhardt, but his notion was innovative and I believe went a long way to saving jazz in this country.

In the early months of 1964, before Ron and I had officially joined the band, but were doing most of the gigs, Wild Bill Davison had made a one-off tour with the Freddy Randall Band. I can't remember the exact circumstances which led to him appearing with us at a new club in a Manchester cellar of a disused warehouse. A man called L C Jenkins, later to be famously known as "Jenks", had opened a sports club on a couple of the lower level floors of the slightly dilapidated, one-time vibrant edifice, with a licensed bar in the basement area. His friend, the afore mentioned Jack, had cajoled him into using it to form a jazz club at the week-ends. It was here at the now famous 'Manchester Sports Guild' that the session took place. More importantly, the session was recorded for publication in the U S A on George Buck's New Orleans-based "Jazzology" label. The album, "Blowing Wild", captured the exciting sound of the extrovert legendary cornetist accompanied by an obviously inspired Alex Welsh and his Band. The room was packed to the 'gunnels' with wildly enthusiastic jazz fans, critics and curious 'walk-ins'. I have a notion that the seeds of the miracle were sown there and then.

Reading between the lines I think Jack must have approached agent, Jack Higgins, of London Management, who had been instrumental in Wild Bill's visit, with an idea to bring over a few more "Legends" who were finding it equally difficult in the States. His first guest was to be the legendary Jack Teagarden, who had been a member of the famous Louis Armstrong All Stars. Unfortunately, the great trombonist was in poor health and declined the invitation. (Now might be an opportune moment to say that "Big T" had been very impressed by Alex's band, who had been the accompaniment on the 1950s tour and by the leader, himself. So much so that he had offered him the trumpet chair in his own outfit back in America.) The next in line on Jack's list was the wonderful Henry "Red" Allen. The rest is now history. In April and May of that year, the first of what was to become a decade of memorable never-to-be- forgotten tours took place. Starting with an unforgettable weekend in the Sports Guild, where Henry appeared with Alex, Humph, Bruce Turner and Sandy Brown, the "show" went on to several provincial venues, causing wide-spread excitement everywhere. The ball was in motion!

During that first remarkable tour, an inspired television producer, Terry Henebery, who had acquired fame from producing "Jazz Club" on radio, instigated a ground-breaking programme on the newly broadcasting BBC2. In June of that wonderful year, "Jazz 625" presented Henry "Red" Allen with the Alex Welsh Band. I think the success of his inspired idea, together with that of Jack Swinnerton, proved to be the nucleus in the preservation of jazz in these islands. The film, one of the few to still exist, has become a favourite on today's "YouTube". It is a little embarrassing now to watch my formative fumbling on the show but, what the heck, I was twenty-two years old and I am justifiably proud to have been part of that historic recording.

As the more discerning of you will remember, or will have been told by older relatives who were present at some of the concerts, the "snowball" rolled itself into a gigantic ice sphere covering the length and breadth of the country. After Henry, who in total visited on four occasions before succumbing to the insidious disease that took him from us, we were enthralled by Wild Bill, Pee Wee Russell, Bud Freeman, Earl Hines, Dicky Wells, Rex Stewart, Eddie Miller and Peanuts Hucko, who all toured with us on several occasions. Others, such as Albert Nicholas, Ben Webster, Vic Dickenson and others joined the infectious party, appearing with other well-known British stars. Audiences swelled in number, unfamiliar faces of critics and journalists appeared from the safety of their private establishments, clubs and venues invested in more seating, better, properly tuned, pianos and decent public address systems, which added to the overall euphoria enjoyed by the band and their guests. Some fine recordings were produced and issued on the "Fontana" label, and as hinted, television producers opened their studio doors to us. We played in concert halls and wooden-walled sports clubs alike. "Steinway" grand pianos were rolled onto creaking, protesting floorboards to accommodate Earl, who was delighted with "Uncle Charlie's" hot dogs at Osterley Rugby Club, where, incidentally the interval music was supplied by the eccentric, Glaswegian, rag-time pianist and "jingle" writer, Ron Geesin

The next change to the band's personnel came as no surprise. Al Gay had made it clear that he was only filling in for a worsening Archie Semple. Having endured enough travelling and all the other demands he had had to contend with as a member of several popular outfits, he just wanted to have his feet on "terra firma", as the saying goes. He had wed young; his wife Rose, having escaped the pressures of the anti-Jewish Nazi campaign in her native Germany, had agreed to a more or less marriage of convenience to assure her safety by becoming a British citizen.

They were blessed with a daughter, Sandra, who was in her early teens and whose formative years he felt he had missed. Having sold a little cafeteria he owned in Gant's Hill in the Essex suburbs of London, he purchased a nursing home in Windsor. Alex was suddenly presented with the problem of who could replace and fill the shoes of two of the best reed players this country ever produced.

Great players like Bruce Turner and Alan Cooper were happy to help when possible but they, of course,m had their own commitments. We found a young clarinettist from the Hampshire area whom Alex was quite excited about, but young Mike Snelling was following a career as a physical training teacher and, after careful consideration and in the light of the current situation for jazz bands, declined Alex's offer to join the band. So where next? The answer came from an unexpected source.

It was at Maidstone on the night of the

ashtray incident that Alex first used John Barnes. A Mancunian by birth, John's musical career had started, like mine, as a drummer in the local Boys' Brigade. He soon went on to clarinet and became known as a very good, Johnnie Dodds-styled player, eventually joining one of the best bands to come out of the Manchester "Scene", the locally famous "Zenith Six".   It is well-documented in jazz lore how he deputized for the Mike Daniels Band in a local fixture and so impressed the leader that he was enticed to London to join the band, with the added carrot of a full-time job in Mike's business dangled in front of him.

Looking to become a full-time musician, John joined the Alan Elsdon Band, in which he became an important contributor to the outfit's popularity, having added to his musical armoury alto and baritone saxophones and a wicked sense of humour in his featured vocals.   Like all the bands affected by the declining popularity of the ill-fated "Trad Boom", Alan's was no different.

I have never asked John why he decided to join Alex's band on that fateful evening in May 1964. I think a feeling that there may be more 'gigs' available or that he looked at it as a chance to move on musically may have been in his decision. Alex had long had the reputation of having one of the best bands around, after all, and it was definitely "earning a stripe" to be askd to join such a good "force" in British Jazz.

At last the band's line-up was complete: Alex; Roy Crimmins; John Barnes; Fred Hunt; Len Hastings; Ron Mathewson and myself ....or so we thought.......

Jim Douglas

Nice shirt, Jim!

Chapter Fifteen

"Lisgar to Mornington"

Although it had been a little nerve-racking at first to follow such great guitarists as Diz and Tony, I had settled into the band pretty well. Inspired and encouraged by such illustrious colleagues, my confidence grew to the point where I felt I was actually contributing to the band and not just fulfilling the role as a rhythm guitarist. My soloing improved with my growing confidence, giving me the satisfying feeling that I was now a fully paid-up member of the famous Welsh Band.

Gigs became more plentiful as interest in the band increased. We seemed to be appearing almost every other week at the 'Sports Guild', the 'Dancing Slipper', the Digbeth Civic Hall in Birmingham, the "Hundred Club" (or 'Jazzshows' as it was then named) and, of course, the "Fishmongers Arms" at Wood Green. There were frequent trips to jazz venues in all corners of the country from Redruth to Redcar, Cambridge to Carlisle, Hastings to Hereford, Grimsby to Aberystwyth and even Aberdeen to Edinburgh and Glasgow.

Back home in our digs, Ron and I settled in to a relaxed, semi--debauched lifestyle of wine, women and song. We partied, played and perpetually had a bit too much to drink. What the Hell! I was twenty-two and Ron just twenty.

It wasn't to last. Ron decided his musical career lay in a more modern jazz direction and decided to leave Alex. We packed in the flat with just a month's notice in which to find alternative accommodation. Ron moved in with friends in

Shepherds' Bush, where he eventually found a permanent flat and where he still lives.

More important than my domestic problems, the question of who would replace one of the best young bassists in the land was uppermost on the band's agenda. Alex asked me if I had any ideas and I told him there was another bassist, another Ron, working in the Edinburgh area, who was well thought of and who I had worked with occasionally. Alex replied:

"We had better give him a try then!"

Ron Rae answered his call positively, travelled to London and moved into the flat with me. First thing after we all mutually agreed that Ron, or Ronnie as he preferred, was right for the band, was to find another place to live.

Just around the corner from Stanwick Road, we found a room in Lisgar Terrace and moved in. Everything was fine at first. We befriended a couple of rhythm and blues musicians, who occupied a room upstairs. Mike and Gerry were seeking success in the blossoming market for that genre.

But Ronnie got more and more restless, eventually owning up that he was really missing his wife and young family. An estate agent and semi-professional trombone player came to the rescue. He gave the bassist the chance to reunite with his family by offering him a furnished, rentable bungalow near Heathrow airport. Ronnie accepted the offer gratefully, his family duly arrived and they took occupation.

Within a week or two the situation imploded! The proximity, firstly, to the airport, with its incessant noise and, secondly, to a pig farm and its unwelcome odours, triggered the unrest. The straw that broke the camel's back was the laughing and jeering at and bullying of his young kids, brought on by their strong Scottish dialect. Margaret, Ron's patient, lovely wife had had enough. Gathering her brood around her, she headed homeward.

I moved into a basement room and shared kitchen at Number Twenty, Mornington Avenue, W14.   Mike and Gerry had taken the entire basement at Number Two. Ronnie moved out of the rented house and joined them. This was to be my first experience of living alone. Let the fun begin!

Jim Douglas

Chapter Sixteen

"Solo Flight"

Ronnie went!   Ron returned and went! Ronnie returned and stayed!

For the next four or five years the band line-up, with the addition of Roy Williams to the trombone chair vacated by an unsettled Roy Crimmins, who had left to further his career in Europe, was at last settled. Influenced by the variety of styles gleaned from accompanying the "Top Table" American guests, the list of which had begun to read like an invitation to a Royal

248

gathering, we began to assemble our own musical "pot pourri". Chicago had supplied Wild Bill, Pee Wee and Bud. Earl Hines showed us how to develop one's roots. Dickie Wells and Rex Stewart introduced the Big Band feeling. Peanuts and Eddie Miller gave us Benny Goodman and Bob Crosbie. Henry Red Allen sailed majestically through all styles in his wonderful way. There were cameo roles from Albert Nicholas, Willie "the Lion" Smith, Sammy Price, Ben Webster and Bill Coleman. And Ruby Braff was Ruby - indefatigable, idiosyncratic, irrepressible, iconic Ruby! All of them added to the band's repertoire. All of them brought us joy. I hope we brought them some pleasure in return. No! That's not right! I know we brought them pleasure! They, to a man, told us so!

My solo flight had led me to the basement of 20 Mornington Avenue, W14, as I have already stated. I had acquired the tenancy to a dampish, doomy-decorated, decrepit den of future fun and frolics from an acquaintance I had befriended in the local pub. Bob Ross was a pianist of enthusiastic endeavour but limited technique, who worked in an afternoon drinking club and several pubs in the area. With his friendship came a new circle of drinking mates of various degrees of dubiousness, some of whom I would certainly not have introduced to my grandmother. They will be involved in the masterplan shortly!

My room was furnished with a double bed, a wardrobe and a sideboard, which had all enjoyed better days and had probably been purchased at nearby North End Road market. The kitchen had two cookers, one fired by gas and of recent manufacture; the other, of dubious age and safety, was electric. I was given the latter but, as my culinary skills were largely confined to omelettes and baked beans on toast, it wasn't too important. Over the years, largely due to economy and the lack of restaurants, other than Chinese or Indian, which opened at convenient hours for jazz musicians, I learned to cook on that old cooker. It proved to have a much more reliable oven than its modern counterpart, so I won in that department. Through the kitchen and just before a door opened onto a below-ground level path, we shared a Victorian loo, complete with a high-level cistern operated by a long chain and a well-worn wooden-seated toilet. All very "under-market", if that is acceptable, but totally what I wanted and at a very affordable rent, which included a clean top sheet every week, the previous one being relegated to the bottom to replace its forerunner, which was then whisked off to the laundry. I moved in my belongings, which consisted mostly of clothes, instruments and records, a turntable and amplifier and a pair of large loudspeakers. With the addition of a couple of favourite pictures to hang on the bare walls, I feathered my new nest.

Fortunately, I didn't have time to be homesick or lonely, although I must admit to becoming occasionally bored with my own company. Equally fortunately, I was befriended by several very nice ladies, who most certainly alleviated most of my moments of boredom. Gill came and slept in my bed. Sue also and Pam and Jane and Janet. Sometimes even in pairs! Betty came for three weeks! Her father had something to do with "Wonderloaf", leaving me to think she expected a bit too much of a rise in my yeast level, but that's unfair and I did love her for at least a couple of weeks! Well, after all, it was the" Swinging Sixties", with its female sexual emancipation and endless parties. With the exception of the "educational, epicurean" Betty, most of my ladies were "just good friends". Ah well!

My mother visited and I slept on the floor. My sister and her family visited and they slept on the floor. Likewise, my good friend Alex Marshall and his clan of campers.

My most important non-staying visitor by far was the indubitable, musically gifted Mister Rae. At some stage, Ronnie had acquired a G I "Gibson Cromwell" guitar on which he had become reasonably adept at working out harmony. On free nights, the bassist would bring his guitar, a "carry-out" of booze and a small amount of brown or green herbal relaxant. On these "spliffing" evenings, he wrote, with a little help from his friend, some of the band's best arrangements. I think "The Shadow of Your Smile" was first, followed by "Shiny Stockings", "Girl Talk" and "Little Darling". Some of them, as testament to his talents, were adopted and recorded by the band and released on various albums and C Ds. "Shiny Stockings", issued on an "Upbeat" BBC CD, features a world class, unforgettable tenor solo by Al Gay. If you haven't heard it, and you are discovering its existence from reading this, close the book, put on your running shoes and head for the nearest stockist. Actually, you can save a lot of effort and time by just buying it on-line now, but, for me, the magic of actually purchasing a longed-for record over the counter is sadly a thing of the past, more's the pity!

I mentioned some dubious characters a paragraph or two ago, with good reason. Returning from a couple of days away with the band, I returned home to find my door forced open and most of my prized possessions, including clothing, the "Agfa" camera I had bought in Germany with which I took the photographs featured in an earlier chapter, and half of my records. The reason I used the word "dubious" is because it all seemed a little bit "planned". During the next week or so, one of my fellow tenants had found a copy of the wonderful Julie London / Barney Kessel album on a stall in North End Road market. She knew it was mine by my signature on the back (a little habit I had adopted) and, realizing how much I treasured my collection, bought it and brought it back to me. I gladly reimbursed her and went out to look for others. I think I found about five or six but, being unable to afford to buy them back, I had to let them go. I informed the Police, of course, but they couldn't help much. I persuaded the landlady to fit a new, more substantial, mortice lock in my door, hoping that future security was guaranteed.

For quite a few weeks I enjoyed almost complete silence, after the departure of the tenants in the ground floor room immediately above me had left. But nothing lasts forever, so I had taken advantage of the temporary situation to play my records a little louder. New tenants eventually arrived in the shape of, I was pleased to note, two academic, serious-looking girls in their twenties (I think the modern description is "nerdy"), who moved in with a viola and a cello.

"Ah, a bit of class!" I thought to myself.

Once again, how wrong could I be? Totally! All day long they scraped away at their viols and all night long fingered and plucked each other's more intimate instruments, with the probable addition of various other forms of devilish imitation apparatus physically attached or hand-held, resulting in tonal screeching by day and atonal, discordant wailing by night. Nice girls but noisy!

My life seemed at last to be conforming to a pattern of sorts. There was enough band work to take care of the rent. There was more than enough musical excitement generated from the same source. My "love life" was more than adequate and I was forming new friendships by the bucketful. I had really settled into my solo existence with "A levels!"

One morning it all came to an end. My solo existence that is! It's amazing how a knock on your door can change things.

The evermore insistent tap-tap-tap unwillingly woke me from my pleasant slumbers. Hungover, inching my way towards the intrusive annoyance, with foul words in my fuzzy brain, ready to be emitted from my coffee- starved mouth, I opened the door to be confronted by the cheery, beret-topped countenance of none other than former seaman, Ronald "Bix" Duff, ex-pianist with Mick Mulligan's "Magnolian" Jazz Band and the "Clyde Valley Stompers" and occasional co-imbiber.

"Sorry tae bother ye Jim, but a wunderred if ye could put me up for a couple o' days? Ah've had a richt Barney wi' the missus and she's chucked me oot!"

You've guessed!   After giving him reasonable excuses why I couldn't, such as: "I only have a double bed", "I'm not here a lot of the time", "the landlady might object" and "I have friends visit from time to time", it became obvious that my words were falling on deaf ears. After my reluctant agreement, he moved in with two suitcases and a bottle of brandy to toast his salvation.

He stayed for six months!

Ronnie "Bix" Duff was a "Teuchter. Anyone born north of Perth, the "gateway to the Highlands", qualified for this description, as those hailing from south of the beautiful city, were known as "Sassenachs". He first opened his lungs in Huntly, near Aberdeen and, for all the years I knew him, hardly ever closed them again. In his high-pitched, very slightly 'Anglified' voice, he held counsel with whomever was "fortunate" to be within earshot. He had discovered jazz in his teens, taking up the trumpet to emulate his namesake hero, a certain Mister Beiderbecke, as well as having piano lessons. His father, it seems, was an indulgent husband to his social-climbing mother, the "Hyacinth Bucket" of the Highlands, if you like. But even his father's patience would snap in the end, when, after what seemed enough to him, at her best-hatted, best-frocked tea parties, he would enter the room and, after placing a finger of one hand in his mouth and one from his other hand in the region of his rectum, he would utter an amazing shout of:

"Finger in mouth, finger in bum – change fingers!"

Leaping into the air he would exchange

the position of his digits. The grossly-embarrassed ladies would hurry home.

It was easy to see where Bix's irreverent sense of adventure came from. His looks were those of his mother but his mischief that of his dad. I had had experience of his "darker" side from his time occupying the piano stool in the "Clydes", of course, which I have touched on in a previous chapter, but just how deep it went was revealed when he moved in. Disguised in satirical humour, his biting observations of less fortunate members of society were sometimes "a little near the mark.," especially after a drink or two. I don't intend belittling him in print, especially when he is no longer here to defend or explain himself, but I did feel a little uncomfortable in his company sometimes.

On the whole, we got along pretty well. Being fellow Scots, we had a great deal in common, especially in the culinary department. Haggis or minced beef, "neeps" and "tatties", leeks, smoked haddock, mutton pies and stoved potatoes ("stovies") became regular new entries on our domestic menu. Like most musicians I have known, he was a fine cook. I suppose it became a necessity to our survival in the days before twenty-four-hour restaurants became a way of life. If he was a good cook, he was a master chef in the boozing department. He had acquired a penchant for a tot of rum from his National Service experience in the Navy, but it didn't end there. Maybe I should tell you of a typical day when, work permitting, we had the same day off. For some reason, it was very often on a Thursday.

The day would begin for me with his gentle awakening shake of my shoulder and a hand holding a cup of coffee, well laced with brandy, presented inches from my face.

"C'mon. Jim – the pub 'll be open in five minutes, we dinna want tae miss oot on oor day aff. Drink up and ah'll see you there!".

After struggling into clean clothes, splashing cold water on my still sleeping face and wondering why I was doing it, I joined him in the Saloon Bar of the pub. The regular alcoholics were already installed, of course. Bix, having joined them, would be holding court, a half-empty pint pot of bitter and a rum chaser on the bar in front of him, with an untouched pint of light and bitter (mine) patiently awaiting its absent imbiber. On arrival, I manfully downed it and ordered another round. By afternoon closing time, I had drunk enough. Our hero, on the other hand, was just entering into the overture of a long Bacchanalian opera, which we would perform over the next twelve hours or so. The "Intermezzo", after a tube train ride to the West End, would be performed in the famous between and after-hours, members-only drinking club, "The Cottage." Like many such clubs, "The Cottage" existed by acquiring a licence to sell alcohol outside of the then legal "opening hours" for public houses and bars. One of the conditions of the licence was the necessary purchase of food to accompany the drinks. For the most part, this consisted of a basic sandwich or salad to accompany the initial beer or spirit, with an over-the-top price attached. On our Thursday "day off," this often constituted breakfast!

At 5.30pm the pubs re-opened. The "Coach and Horses" on the corner of Charing Cross Road and Old Compton Street would be our next stop. A pint or two in that well-known jazz pub and off up Soho's Dean Street to Acker Bilk's recently opened "Capricorn Club". Tired of ale, Bix would "do the optics." Working from bottom left to top right, he would sample each and every spirit in order.

By 11.00pm, I would be really beginning to feel the effects of booze and fatigue, even though I had reined myself in quite a lot by then and even cheated, by having the odd bag of crisps or nuts. Not our hero! Catching a tube to Earls' Court, we would head for the then famous "Naraine" Indian restaurant. To wash down our

Vindaloo, Bix would order a half-bottle of Chianti. Back in our room, it was, of course, mandatory to have a coffee and brandy "night cap" before retiring - he visually none the worse for wear, me a farting, snoring hangover in the making.

Eventually Bix moved out. I don't think he went home to his family - in fact I know he didn't. Some other gentle soul probably took pity on him and in the process, patiently endured his eccentricity. It hadn't all been negative though! During his 'visit' he taught me several things, both in music theory and in general 'lifemanship'. He made me frustrated some of the time. He made me laugh a lot of the time. He made me almost cry on occasion but, most of the time, he made me glad to have known him. Our paths crossed spasmodically over the next few years. On one occasion, we shared a stand at the Tufnell Park Tavern. I was glad to see him, but noticed how emaciated he had become. He had let his now-grey hair, around a balding monk-like crown, grow shoulder length. When I asked where he was living, he replied that he had found a cosy room near Waterloo Station. I never went there so I can't tell how cosy it was. Not long after that, I heard he had died. He had reached the respectable three score years and ten expected of mankind in the Biblical sense. Even a little bit longer! If I had been a betting man, I would have laid odds he wouldn't achieve anything like that. I am truly glad to hypothetically have lost that bet.

After Bix left, my lifestyle of wine, women and song continued. Something was missing though! I took a long look at myself and decided that, at the grand old age of twenty- four, it may be time to consider settling down. I had no one in mind, although a few of my favourites had offered themselves as candidates in the metamorphosis going on in my head. I need not have worried! My whole life was about to change. Whether for better or worse, time would be the judge.

Chapter Seventeen

"In Sickness and Health"

On my own again, I decided to redecorate my room. The landlady seemed amazed and, at the same time, delighted, by my offer. To help, she waived my rent for a couple of weeks and I got on with the job. After changing the whole colour scheme, I rearranged the furniture, achieving, in doing so, a bit more space. I took a step back, took a good look at my handiwork and gave myself a small pat on the back. Everything was just fine – even the "Vivaldi" sisters upstairs seemed to have learned to restrain their banshee-like screaming to times when they knew I was out!   Or maybe I had just "Grown Accustomed to their Phases" sexual and musical. Bring on the dancing girls, I thought. I was ready to add variations to my repertoire.

Indeed, for a few months, this is exactly what happened. I don't know why or when I began to feel the need of regular companionship. Maybe, subconsciously, I missed Bix's incessant prattle, especially during the daytime, or was it that the "Sixties" had stopped "Swinging" a little for me? I do remember thinking maybe it was time to settle down as, after all, I was approaching the grand old age of twenty-five!

In 1965/66, the tours with our American guests were taking us all around the country. Clubs in the cities and larger towns had all clamoured to offer engagements. Like a welcome mini-epidemic, smaller clubs, theatres and concert halls were jumping on the bandwagon in an effort to be part of history-in-the-making. Jazz buffs who had resigned themselves to their armchairs to enjoy their favourites on modern "Hi-fi" systems, dragged their arses to performances in places they hadn't supported for years. Critics who rarely had much to say about British bands came out of the woodwork, to be seen rubbing shoulders with their idols, even condescending to talk to and write about previously, largely-ignored home-grown musicians. Perhaps, on reflection, I'm being a little unfair to both parties! After all, they were just as excited as we were to hear and meet their heroes in the flesh and, what's more, we had the added pleasure, if that's a strong enough word, to be playing and virtually living with them.

The aforementioned venues went out of their way to accommodate us. Promoters such as Graeme Bayley at Codsall, near Wolverhampton, Steve Duman at the "George" in Morden, Surrey, Jim Chambers at the "Pheasant" in Carlisle and Yurek (whose unpronounceable to me Polish surname has long deserted my memory), at the New Orleans Club in Newcastle upon Tyne, were some of the more regular ones to take our package.

Digressing slightly, it would be remiss of me not to include John Barnes's recollection of a telephone call he once made to the latter regarding some article he had left behind:

"New Orleans Cloob!"

a voice announced;

"Hello Yurek, John Barnes here!"

"How did you know zis was me?"

was the surprised reply!

All over the country, it was the same story. We appeared in Birmingham, Manchester, Nottingham, Liverpool and London, of course, but also in smaller cities like Coventry, Sheffield, Chester, Bristol and Bath, Chichester, Norwich and Leeds. Towns we seldom visited suddenly became interested, necessitating travel to the likes of Reading, Rugby and Rhyl. North of the Border we played in Edinburgh, Glasgow, Aberdeen and Dundee. The entire country was our newly-opened oyster and our music the pearl everyone seemed to want. Great times!

But the excitement didn't follow me into my more- and more lonely room. One minute of being the centre of attention was followed by my looking at the four, albeit, newly-decorated, walls or into the barren wasteland that was my view from the little basement window. Recordings and alcohol helped, of course, but the need to converse with someone with the same interests became more and more important to me simply because of the lack of suitable "candidates for the position."

In the Autumn months of 1964, a chance introduction to a young lady changed my whole situation. It happened in the "Fishmongers Arms" at Wood Green, where the band still played regularly on Sunday evenings. For those of you unfamiliar with Alex's lifestyle, suffice to say he enjoyed ladies' company. In fact, he was a downright flirt and womanizer, with "conquests" all around the jazz scene.

This particular evening at the aforementioned club, one of his friends, a lady called Joyce, came to see the band in general and Alex in particular, accompanied by a tall, blonde-haired friend, with blue eyes and dimples in her cheeks. She was introduced to me as Jacquie and she told me they had travelled from Luton, a town in Bedfordshire famous for the Hat Trade, the invention of the "Straw Boater" and Vauxhall Motors. There was also a small airport (although nothing like it is today). We seemed to get on well and I asked her if we could meet again, even offering to get a train to her neck of the woods, if she preferred. She preferred and we met up several times. Eventually she visited me. We went out in London to wine, dine and be merry resulting in her missing the last train home and falling into bed with me at the end of the evening. This was not what you are imagining! We remained "just good friends" for quite a while. As our relationship grew, so did our fondness for each other. I met her parents, Doug and Jeanne and slept on their sofa when in Luton.

One day, I brought up the subject of marriage. I didn't go down on one knee but must have asked nicely enough to hear her reply of "Yes please!" The next few months were like a whirlwind of planning, compiling invitation lists and general excitement in anticipation of our future together. Jacquie was nineteen and I was twenty-five when we tied the knot at St Joseph's Church in Luton on the 26th August 1967. We held the reception in a country mansion owned by an ex-army Officer turned restaurateur. My family and the entire band and their wives and children attended and we had a bag-piper, Donald Finlayson and peacocks on the lawn. My best man, my brother, Ian and I wore kilts in the traditional way, which may have accounted for some murmurs we heard when we ascended to a minstrel gallery to read the telegrams.

After the reception, which ran a bit over, as usual, Jacquie and I changed, to be whisked at a hundred miles an hour in good friend, LaurIe Ridley's Jaguar motor car to a theatre in London to watch "Fiddler on the Roof", starring Miriam Karlin and Topol in the leading roles.

The sun had shone! Champagne had flowed! The skirl of the pipes had vied with the screeching of the peacocks. Mothers beamed, brothers laughed, my sister cried and toddlers played hide-and-seek among the shrubs, giving their grateful parents a little time to themselves. It was a splendid day, captured in the smiles of all in the accompanying picture, taken by Doug, who had a field day indulging in his favourite pastime, photography. Don't we all look so young? The usual suspects read from left to right: Lennie Hastings, Ron Rae, my brother Ian, Roy Williams, Chief Culprit and his Henchwoman, Al Gay, Donald Finlayson, Fred Hunt, Alex Welsh and John Barnes.

Bless them all!

Chapter Eighteen

"Bricks and Mortar "

How can I describe twelve years which began like a "Mills and Boon" romantic novel and ended in deceit, disillusionment and dark despair in one short chapter? There seems no other way for me to go other than to make light of it, sweep everything under an imaginary carpet and, in keeping with the overall purpose of this book, carry on relating the development of my jazz career during these eventful years. But, rather than just totally dismissing out of hand what turned out to be a decade of friendship and fondness for each other and which happily coincided with probably the band's most prolific and profitable era, I will be happy to paint you an impressionistic picture of our time together to broaden the general landscape of my life at that time.

Our first home was an upstairs furnished flat in Fifth Cross Road, Twickenham, Middlesex. As a pure matter of coincidence, it wasn't a million miles from that of Len and Janet Hastings in Chertsey Road and on a convenient bus route to the town centre, with its shops and railway station. Close to the river at Strawberry Vale where Roy Williams had once moored an ill-fated boat and television quiz presenter, Michael Miles, resided, the area was as picturesque as convenient.

Jacquie had found a good secretarial job with a Soho-based import company and commuted there daily. While she was at work, I learned to drive to Government Standards, duly passing my test. The band had helped fund me in my project, with a view to my taking over a large chunk of bandwagon driving duties. I obliged by sharing the driving of Len's little 5cwt Ford van, which had been acquired to transport most of the larger instruments and equipment. I have told of our adventures together in my previous book, so I will not add to that, but just add that the 'Lenvan,' as it became known, provided Alex with a genuine nightmare of expense and trepidation as to whether we would arrive at the gig on time, or even at all. Somehow we always did. Mind you, Fred's 'Zodiac' wasn't much better, resulting in a two-way stretch of the nerves and sinews of all concerned.

A few happy months went by. Unfortunately, some jars of soothing ointment often turn out to have a dead fly in them and ours was no exception. The ground floor flat was occupied by the son of the owner and his young family. It seemed that my lifestyle of coming home late from gigs was disturbing their peace. We were asked very nicely if we could look for somewhere else to stay. On Jacquie's mentioning the situation at work, one of the three brothers by whom she was employed, informed her that he had heard there was an unfurnished flat for rent near where he lived in the Falloden Way area of East Finchley. It would be more expensive, but she could save on travelling expenses by sharing his car to work. Even better, if I drove them there, I could have the car on occasion. After legal contracts were signed and deposits made, we moved in.

The flats were, I suppose, of the "Art Deco" 1930's period - all brick, with metal-framed, small-paned windows of the forever-rusty style. The flats were on two floors, one above another, over a street-level parade of shops. Falloden Way was part of the A1, London to Edinburgh trunk road. Our little stretch was imaginatively named "Market Place" and we had number three. It was to prove invaluable in every aspect of our varied lifestyles and needs. For my part, being so near to the two main roads north out of London, it became a central pick-up point for the band. For Jacquie, she was a little nearer her parents, had little trouble getting to work and was just around the corner from where her boss lived in Ossulton Way.

Raymond Meller was the youngest of three Jewish brothers, the others being Norman and Percy. In the old style of respect, they liked their staff to use "Mister" in front of their first names. It soon became clear to me that, in return for his unquestionable generosity, 'Mister' Raymond expected a few little favours in return. I found myself cutting his lawn, touching up paintwork, running little errands and even baby-sitting his three Belgian Griffin dogs. As time went on, we were invited to Percy's sons' Bar mitzvahs and I drove them to the family graves in Edmonton on the occasion of Yom Kippur. With the occasional personal use of his car, it really was an idyllic situation.

The only drawback was my increasing need to be away from home, leaving my young wife alone in the evening. She had friends visit her from Luton from time to time, but they were scant substitutes for a husband. The solution presented itself one Saturday morning on a family visit to her parents, by a chance utterance from Doug, that the construction company, "Wimpey" were building some new houses on an estate in the Leagrave area of Luton. They comprised both terraced and semi-detached "chalet" style, three and four-bedroomed houses, as well as a planned infant school close by. There were good reasons to consider it worth a visit to the site, with a view to maybe even buying a place of our own. Firstly, the rent in our Hampstead Garden Suburb flat was at least twice what mortgage repayments would be for property in Luton. Secondly, we would get on the "housing ladder" and, as a third consideration, Luton offered nearby access to the M1 motorway, the A5 trunk road at Dunstable and the A1 at Baldock. There was also a healthy amateur jazz scene in the area. But the final consideration was the site's close proximity to Jacquie's parents, grandparents, other members of her family and, of course, her close friends, which would guarantee company for her when I was touring.

We visited the site, were impressed by the show houses and the surrounding area, with another feature being its close proximity to the railway station at Leagrave, from which commuting to London would prove easy. We secured a mortgage and bought a corner piece of mud, chalk and rubble, on which our first terraced home would be built. Over the next few months, we visited our property regularly, never failing to be excited by the rapidly-growing edifice which was to be our future home. In 1971, we moved in!

We shared our lives there for the next eight years. We painted and decorated, furnished and gardened our brand new shell, found good neighbours and friendships and, apart from the "man of the house" having a slightly eccentric occupation as an itinerant musician, settled into suburbia.

There were, naturally, the usual marital

"ups and downs", "tiffs" and rows, ambitions and disappointments, mistakes and successes. Most of the rows were probably caused by my honest mistakes and lack of care, such as when I did a hot wash with a navy blue sock in it, resulting in Jacquie's usually pristine white underwear turning a shade of electric blue or when, after careful planning and selection between us, I managed to order, have delivered and fitted throughout our open plan living room, stairs and landing, a carpet of the wrong colour. In my defence, I argued that the book sample looked entirely different under the strip lighting in the showroom, but I was judged to be eligible to receive the "rolling pin", anyway and subsequently sentenced to a complete re-painting programme to cover my erroneous effort.

The 'ups' in the first few years were manifested in the slightly better standard of living we enjoyed from lower financial outgoings and increased income, thanks to Jacquie's substantial earnings, even after travelling costs and my increased volume of work. The "downs" meant we were actually seeing less of each other because of our commitments. What time we did have together was, on the most part, enjoyable but, apart from dinner parties with neighbours, we were going our own ways more and more. Jacquie spent a lot of time in the evenings sewing and dressmaking, which had been her mother's occupation, while, in the daytime, I rediscovered the game of golf.

Born in the golfing area of the links of the Firth of Forth, I had indulged a little as a schoolboy. While living at Mornington Avenue I had, with the help of smokers in the band and other sources, collected cigarette coupons and 'Green Shield Stamps' sufficient to acquire a basic set of clubs, which I put into use at the municipal course at Richmond. By the time I had moved to Luton, my game had improved enough for regular visits to the 'South Beds Golf Club', where I was welcomed by members and visitors alike as good enough to join in their daily games. I played with such notables as Richard

Coogan, the Bedfordshire Champion, 'Ten Goal' Joe Payne, the notable legend of the Luton Town Football Club and several stars appearing at Dunstable's 'Caesar's Palace' nightclub, such as Tony Christie and Val Doonican.

Our blossoming friendship with two sets of neighbours led us to decide to accompany them on a package holiday to Fuengirola, near Torremollinos, in Spain. This was our second trip to the Iberian Peninsula. Both holidays were different for substantial reasons. Both provided a rest and a great deal of fun, but the first was spoiled slightly for me by someone I couldn't take my eyes off and the second probably furnished me with the memory of one the worst days of my life. A third, ill-advised and still to be paid for after a couple of weeks in Glyfada, near Athens, drove what proved later to be the first nail in the coffin which contained our marriage. Let me explain!

Chapter Nineteen

"A Donkey Serenade"

In 1968, a year or so into our marriage, a young lady called Margaret Collins came to a gig in Pinner, near Harrow in North East London. Slim as a reed, wearing a short, black dress, she looked stunning. The first thing I saw of her as I looked up from the fret board on my guitar was her legs. From her black sling back shoes up to the hem of the dress a few inches above her knees, she possessed two of the finest, most elegant legs I had ever seen. But it didn't stop at the hem! Following the line of the dress upwards, I noticed how slim she was. Then I saw her face which was lit up by a wide fleshy mouth which had stretched itself into a gleeful, beaming grin. With her green eyes twinkling, here was a portrait that deserved a perfect frame. It was already in place in her crowning glory, her hair. Cut elfin-short, which complimented her features, her hair was of the deepest natural Titian red I had ever seen. Neither ginger nor carroty, it was the colour dye manufacturers would give thousands of pounds to emulate and young ladies, desirable to equal such a tone, spend similar sums to fulfil their dreams. What's more, she seemed to be enjoying the music we were playing.

What am I thinking, I chided myself – a newly married man with a lovely wife looking at other girls? If any or all of you hot-blooded men had been there that evening, I think your heads and minds would also have been turned. One person I knew would have noticed her was old beady-eyed, womanising Alex Welsh. He noticed her, of course and, true to his colours, had left the band to play a quintet number as he, having spotted her coming from the direction of the toilets, took up a position where she would have to walk past him. He greeted her with a suggestive "Hello!". Cheeky bugger! Ah well. I thought to myself, *que sera, sera,* behave yourself, it's none of your business. A month later, on our return visit, having noticed she was once again present, he approached her at the bar and invited her to have a drink with him. The bait was cast! Now let's see if the fish would bite. He asked her if she had liked the music the band had played. On her reply that she had indeed enjoyed herself very much, he said she should come to the '100 Club' and asked for her telephone number to enable him to inform her of our next booked performance there. He telephoned her the very next day. Sure enough she turned up at the gig with a friend. The rest is history. Maggie and Alex were about to set off on a journey across stormy waters over the next decade or so in which I was, of course, part of his 'navy', never realising that another, longer, journey was to transpire for Maggie and me in times to come.

I'm jumping the gun again, aren't I?

In August 1969, Alex and Maggie, Jacquie and I went on holiday together to an embryonic resort called Cala Millor in Majorca. We had a great break, although it was noticeable that we did go our separate ways a lot of the time. Jacquie was a prolific sunbather, spending hours tanning herself, while I had to have frequent trips in to shady spots, such as beach bars, etcetera. Alex and Maggie found other pursuits which, of course, were none of my business, except for one fly in the ointment which had begun to buzz around in my head – when we were together, I couldn't take my eyes off her.

On an excursion to the famous 'Caves of Drach', we were entertained by a charming, but very out of tune, string quartet on a boat, playing the not quite beautiful but, nevertheless, haunting 'Barcarole'. After a visit to the nearby pearl factory, we went shopping and Alex bought an acoustic guitar, which turned out to be very good value for the tenner he paid for it and which became an integral part of the rest of our holiday. Maggie, coming from a musical family who liked jazz, knew all the right tunes and could hold a melody with her attractive singing voice. Together with Alex's ability to harmonise and my accompaniment, we had several great late night sessions.

One morning, over an 'English' breakfast in the appropriately named 'Manchester Arms', we decided to hire a couple of donkey-drawn carts to explore the town, with the double purpose of perhaps being able to buy a 'continental' electric adaptor for Jacquie's hairdryer. I can't remember if we were successful or not, but I do know that we decided to tie up the carts while we explored. Alex and Maggie found a little bar to have a drink, while we shopped. Suddenly a commotion in the street drew our attention. People shouting, laughing and pointing made us look towards our tethered animals. Amid a cacophony of jangling bells and "ee- awing", Alex's donkey had decided to sit down and refused to get up. Eventually, with much cajoling and straining, and with the 'help' of the town's only two policemen, who, in less than friendly terms had explained that we were not supposed to stop the carts, we managed to get the wretched animal back on four pins and re-attached to his cart. We decided enough was enough and after remounting our seats, headed back to the stable. Also staying at our hotel, (I should have mentioned it before), was the epitome of the English holidaymaker in the shape of a small, dapper, pencil-moustached, middle aged man. Typically attired in 'Hawaiian' shirt, long shorts, ankle socks and sandals with a knotted handkerchief on his head, he was accompanied literally by two fat ladies.

As we were approaching our destination, about two or three hundred yards away, this very person and his entourage, having had the same idea as ourselves, passed us on their way out. Wedged between his companions, he waved and shouted "Hello". We returned their greetings and carried on. Suddenly, Jacquie let out a "whoop" and burst into fits of laughter. Alex and

Maggie, who were in front of us, turned to see what was happening, immediately "falling about" at what they saw. Behind them, Jacquie and I were trying to hold back the tears while pointing behind us. There, coming up in the rear was the poor fellow's donkey cart, two fat ladies and all. I don't know if the donkey had thought to itself, "Sod this for a lark" or what, but, ignoring all the coercion, yelling and threats coming from its passengers, it had decided to turn around and was following us home! All three units arrived back together and, I'm happy to report, order was re-instated and the little man and his companions set out again. We dried the tears from our eyes and headed to the bar. It would be a while before I'd have any more encounters with donkeys, I decided!!

Chapter Twenty

"Travails with a Donkey"

I suppose I could have titled this chapter 'To Hell and Back' but, though fitting, it is better reserved for an adventure I endured on our second holiday. Jacquie and I, some good friends and close neighbours, Mike and Chris Radford and Mike and Gill Willment, had decided over dinner one evening to book a fortnight in Fuengirola. All in all, it was a great holiday with sun, sand and smiles. We befriended a couple of Germans there, Gaby and Erwin, strangers not only to us but also to each other. Gaby had been born in the Eastern Sector behind the Iron Curtain but somehow had managed to escape several times, only returning for family reunions, while Erwin, a Berliner, had played professional football for his City's teams. We all got on wonderfully well! All the diversity of our life-styles, jobs hobbies, likes and dislikes were forgotten as we relaxed and had a ball. We hadn't even bothered to book any excursions away from the hotel, such was the enjoyment we were having. Except one, that is.

Looming large for me was the spectre of a donkey descent to a farm/orange-grove for a 'Paella' lunch. The evening before, for some reason or another, knowing full well we had a six a.m. coach call, we stayed up revelling until about four in the morning. I then did the most stupid thing I could have done by going to bed for an hour. Of course I had a hangover! I had the mother of hangovers! Even my hangover had a hangover!

At six o' clock, green-faced and with an

orchestra of a thousand percussionists banging away in my head, I mounted the coach which was to transport us to the 'burro' stables where I would be acquainted with my long eared, furry friend-for-the-day. I remember, as we sped along, leaning my throbbing temple against the cool glass of the coach's window but the vibration from the engine only made things worse. Ushered into a reception area on arrival we were offered coffee. They didn't say it would contain goat's milk. After one sip, excusing myself, I headed for the toilet for my first but by no means only, gastric ejaculation of the day. Emerging at last from my exertions in the 'Khasi', the first thing that greeted me was old 'Phoebus' himself, taking of his night cap and donning his summer bonnet.

"Fuck off, Sun! You're the last thing I need today!

I heard myself say as I gloomily joined my fellow riders-to-be, feeling as fragile as a piece of Dresden China in a commercial dishwasher.

It was at this point that 'Old Nick' himself, in the guise of the donkey breeder, appeared in the door-way to tell us our equine transporters were all fed, watered and ready for us. Grudgingly I was led to my straw hatted, long eared beast of burden (the burden was mostly on my part) and told to mount. The look on Jack's or perhaps Jenny's face exactly mirrored my abject own. I could just imagine the poor animal dreaming of a better way of life than this.

Once uncomfortably mounted I felt for stirrups. There were none! All I wanted was to put my feet down on something solid and all I had was hot dry air. So we set off! My gang thought it would be better if I took the lead so they could keep an eye on me. Just in front of me was a small donkey buried under the fleshy buttocks of a large lady who I remember was incessantly singing. I imagined I'd be a little weary of the tuneless song she was humming by the time we arrived at our destination at least half an hour away, at the foot of what felt like the descent of Everest. I need not have worried! No sooner had we started, than her ass 'let off!" Not her! Her donkey, and it continued farting almost in my face for the whole journey. By the time we dismounted, my nostrils were permanently permeated by the scent of digested, fermenting hay and my shoes had become deep-sea diver's lead-filled boots.

I couldn't face the 'Sangria' refreshment offered after we had dismounted and after making my excuses, sloped off to find somewhere shady and quiet to 'get my head down.' I found an ideal spot in the orangery a few hundred yards away. Away from booze! Away from the smoke of the fishy-smelling paella the organisers were preparing for lunch. Away from the sun! Away from everything but welcome repose! So I thought! I had just settled down with an orange from the tree I was lying under, squeezing the refreshing juice onto my welcoming tongue, when a workman arrived. Just within sight of me, but oblivious of my presence, he lowered his trousers and presented me with a solid version of what the donkey in front had been trying to achieve. Gastric ejaculation number two! I struggled to my feet and headed back to where the others were still quaffing sangria as if it would run out at any moment. I was just thinking that the 'hair of the dog' might be the answer when I noticed Mike Willment's hands, glass and lips. All three were crawling with ants! Gastric Ejaculation number three!

As the day went on, I was able to keep down a couple of gins and tonic which gave me enough appetite to try a little plain food. Gradually I could just about face the return ascent to the stable andthe welcoming coach ride back to the hotel. The next day I still felt pretty shaky so I abstained from alcohol once more. I ask you, a Scotsman on holiday off the booze? On the following day I joined the two Mikes at what we called the 'Bridge Bar' a little pub on the beach. When asked what I wanted I replied that a 'Coca Cola' would be nice. Unknown to me the crafty buggers laced it heavily with 'Bacardi' rum. Being thirsty, I downed it in one swallow! In half an hour I was right as rain and raring to go.

What remained of the holiday passed without event except perhaps for a horse ride where I fell over my horse's head as it lowered it to graze and Chris, bra-less under a Madras cotton blouse, returned with bleeding nipples after her horse had bolted.

We returned home, in need of a good holiday

Chapter Twenty-one

"Trojan Horse"

There was nothing funny about our third holiday to Glyfada near Athens. I don't remember why or how this vacation ever came about but, now, reading between some well-defined lines, I should have spotted the obvious hints that things were changing in our marriage. There was plenty of romance in, for me, rediscovering the wonderful Acropolis, with its attendant giant butterflies and seeing it illuminated from a café as we ate 'kleftika' and drank 'retsina' wine, the breaking of plates after joining a knee-bruising 'Zorba'-style dance and the walk through the market where Jacquie's bottom was pinched black and blue - but the early signs were there, manifested in the lack of romance between us. I befriended a guitar-owning Nashville-residing, American who showed me tricks from the 'Gran' Old Opry' and I in return introduced him to Django, Charlie Christian and Eddie Lang. We took to spending the afternoons 'jamming' after Jacquie had excused herself to have a siesta. From what I know now, was she really sleeping? She certainly wasn't sleeping with me! That had gradually ceased! I did think a romantic break would rekindle what dying embers might be left under the surface. I even started to wonder if something was wrong with me or if I had done something to turn her off me. I have to say at this stage that, on most occasions in the less than recent past, the 'earth' had rarely 'moved' but, in my naiveté, I believed things would improve with time.

The holiday was largely a disappointment

for me. On our return, things fell back into their normal pattern– my touring all over the place and her commuting daily to London. Friends forever without frills. How stupid and blinkered I must have been when she asked me if I minded if she went on a skiing holiday on her own and I said I didn't! How could I when I was away so much? Then she got interested in tennis and was invited to join a 'friend' who had two tickets for Centre Court at Wimbledon. How did I not read the signs when I saw her on television sitting next to him? So it went on! She suddenly became bosom buddies with Fred Hunt's wife, Brenda, citing sewing as the common denominator. "Funny", I thought, as she had never liked Brenda that much. (I had also found her to be a troublesome, meddling, busybody, always gossiping and cynically running people down.)

I have to admit, at this stage, that celibacy was not, at the tender age of thirty-something, in my master plan. I had never considered myself a 'lady's man' – in fact the opposite – but, tired of being rebuffed, I became curious to know why. I started to flirt a little. During visits to the Germanys, my self-assurance was reborn. On trips to the East, I was virtually propositioned after several concerts and, in the West, I found a lady who might have changed my whole life if I had found the courage to turn my back on my status quo. C was married to a musician who played the same instruments as me. They lived in "Thistle town" on the Rhine. The first time I met them was at a jazz club where we were appearing. Every time I looked up, a pair of piercing eyes were burning into mine. In the interval, I approached the bar and found her by my side. In almost perfect English, she told me how much she and her husband were enjoying my playing – especially the banjo. At the end of the session, they invited me to their home for a night cap. The night cap transformed itself into a full-blown ten-gallon hat and I ended up staying the night. The next day, left alone together, C and I developed our relationship. Over the next couple of years or so, this blossomed into a full-blown affair. We met in Germany and back here in England. I knew then that my marriage was virtually over. Jacquie must have felt the same. It was obvious she too had long ago found someone else. We carried on with the pretence, largely because we liked each other. There was also Jacquie's religious upbringing to consider and what it would mean to her Catholic mother, if we parted. At the Easter weekend of 1979 the 'shit hit the fan'! Sitting quietly at breakfast on the Saturday morning, she dropped the bombshell that she had found someone else and wanted a divorce to marry him.

I had expected it for some time, of course! The roles could even have been reversed! It still came as a shock - a bit like walking carefully through a minefield, where you know where most of the traps are hidden and suddenly stepping on one accidentally, I suppose. In the silence that followed, I realised I had to get to Wavenden for The Dankworth's Spring Jazz do. Numb and confused at the same time, I must have gone there, but I remember nothing of the event at all. On my return home, Jacquie and I discussed our next move. That's when the atomic reactor blew!

During the earlier years of our almost normal relationship, it had surprised both of us that Jacquie had never become pregnant. Having been born with mumps, I had occasionally considered that I might be sterile, but had never been 'tested'. What emerged from the 'fallout' of the explosion just about 'put the tin hat' on the whole affair. She revealed she was indeed expecting his child. On experiencing the same lack of success with him, Jacquie had undergone tests, found some small abnormality which was soon put right and had 'fallen' immediately. In trying to digest this revelation, I asked about who he was, etcetera. She said his name was George, that she had met him in London some five years before and an affair had developed. She then told me he was thirty years older than her, a grandfather with a wife and married children!

There was no way back. All the bridges had been burned. We decided I could live in the house until the divorce was finalised and it could be sold. She was entitled by law to half of the value.

It was almost twenty years to the month from when I had become a professional musician to that awful day. I really needed to take stock of everything, weigh up my options and decide where my future path lay. With Alex's health noticeably beginning to deteriorate and the completely different personnel of the band, recreating a new but, in my opinion, retrograde, sound, I wondered if it was time to pack my bags and once more re-cross Hadrian's Wall, this time for good. I decided to give it the time the divorce took and the house was sold before I made up my mind.

It had been twenty years of fun, fantasy, fears and friendships - two decades of change in my life and in the lives of almost everyone globally. Mankind had developed space travel and walked on the moon. The world had shrunk with the inevitable development of air travel and telecommunications. On the music side, it had started for me with 'Skiffle', then the 'Trad Boom', the natural progression to Alex's band and the arrival of the American jazz legends, but sadly we had lost Louis and the 'Duke'. Domestically, the ability to purchase one's home, own a car and travel abroad on package holidays had all taken place. Positively or negatively, the world was changing for everyone and I was no exception.

Chapter Twenty-two

"Double Ending"

The pattern the band followed could be described as parallel to that of my marriage. My courtship with the band had started around 1963 and my joining cemented in 1964. Both were slightly earlier than my marriage in 1967, as you will, by now, realise. The final end to the band came with Alex's untimely death in 1982, slightly outlasting the duration of my marriage to Jacquie.

During these eighteen years of my association with the band, I met hundreds of keen jazz fans, made scores of friendships, some lasting to this day, visited some wonderful villages, towns and cities both here in our island homeland and further afield in the countries which constitute the continent of Europe, as well as even farther away in America and Africa.

Many of the more famous venues we visited and the stars we accompanied have been remembered in my first book, *Tunes, Tours and Travelitis,* but not all the anecdotes were included in it. So, with your kind permission and with that of those I am pleased to acknowledge personally, I will recall one or two which will live in my memory forever, to bring the curtain down on 'Book Two'.

I will begin with a story that happened before I joined but will 'set the mood', I hope:

Trombonist, Roy Crimmins, before turning professional, had an apprenticeship in the Civil Service. As an office boy, he literally started at the bottom, on the ground floor of a several-storey block. Part of his job was to collect waste paper from the many offices and, by service lift, deposit them in a large bin stored in a room at the top of the building. One day, on looking out the window he realised that he could see into the dressing rooms of a ladies' fashion shop. Well, as most young, hot-blooded men would have done, he found more excuses to visit the window. It all came to an end quite unexpectedly one afternoon, when he heard the lift ascending. Realising it was going to stop at the room, he looked around for somewhere to hide. The only place was the waste receptacle, which was just large enough to crouch in. In he got! To his dismay, he heard the clip-clop of his manageress's high-heeled shoes coming straight towards him. On opening the lid of the bin and shocked by what she saw, she let out a scream:

"What on earth are you doing in there, Crimmins?"

she asked, after catching her breath.

"Handing in my notice!"

came the reply.

One of the countries we visited was Saudi Arabia in 1971. We were invited by the Arabian American Oil Company, or 'Aramco', to use its acronym, to celebrate the New Year in their three departments. Before we left, we were booked to play in Manchester. In those days John Barnes's mother was still alive and had attended the gig in the company of John's two sisters, Marian and her husband Hope, and Mary with her husband Bill. At one stage the reed man asked his mother:

"Hey, Mam, guess where we're playing on New Year's Eve? Saudi Arabia!"

Without a hint of surprise, she replied

"Oh - Bill's on nights."

The trip in itself is memorable for several amusing reasons. The first concerns me and a litre-bottle of duty-free whisky, which I had purchased with the certain knowledge that where we were going was "dry" in more than one sense. At the time, I favoured a 'Fender' amplifier, in which the valves were suspended from the chassis. To prevent accident on the flight, I removed them and placed them in the carrier bag with my whisky. You've guessed! At the check-in, I dropped the bag and smashed the lot! On arrival at Aramco, I explained my predicament to one of our hosts. Without further ado and to my disbelief and undying gratitude, he took me to the stores and replaced every single valve at no expense.

"Just as well you got an American amp!",

he said and laughed heartily!

"See you for cocktails at six!"

The trip was a roaring success. The Saudi government had turned a blind eye on the use of home-distilled alcohol they called "Blue Flash." The manufacture of this in itself had caused several accidents in the haste to mature the end product. It saved our lives – especially those of Len and Alex, who were a little more dependent than the rest of us on good old "Mother's Ruin". On the return flight, we were scheduled to have two stops. The first was Bahrain, where we were allowed to purchase 'booze' in the duty-free shop. By the time we re-boarded and landed at our second destination, Cairo, Len had imbibed his fair share of his juniper-based 'friend'. I remember watching him descend the ramp and head for the transit lounge, laughing as he went. He wasn't laughing on his return! Taken suddenly short for the more substantial kind of toilet visit, he had found some out-of-the-way closet and used it. It was, of course, after the event, that he noticed a lack of toilet paper. Looking around for a substitute, he spotted a hose pipe curled up in one corner, still attached to a tap. Holding it and pointing it in the appropriate direction, he turned it on. A ferocious stream of water gushed out, completely soaking him from his sandaled feet to his now drowned, rat-like toupee. His multi-coloured shirt changed colour, his 'Leichner Number 5' was running down his face and water squelched from his toes. Alex had to use all his powers of persuasion for him to be allowed back on the plane. As he later remarked:

"I should have left him there! At least

it would have stopped the arguments!"

To facilitate my declining memory, I will be better served if I associate some of my ramblings with unforgettable places and venues we visited. Here I intend to just let my ageing brain divulge incidents that I hope are both interesting and amusing. I will begin by minimalizing an occurrence at a pub called the 'Hardinge Arms' where I was the star of the show, I'm afraid.

For one reason or another, the rhythm section that evening included on drums the late Tony Allen, who had also driven the band bus. During the course of the evening, I had spotted (I was still single, Your Honour!) a very attractive French au pair girl with the charming name, Armelle. By the end of the gig, my schoolboy French had, with all its seductive undertones, succeeded in our leaving the pub together, finding a spot in the car park (I ask you!) where we could develop International Relations, and were just getting down to it, as they say! Suddenly to my horror and disbelief, we were illuminated by the headlights of the band coach. I suppose Tony thought it amusing, but I was less than delighted. I have often performed under spotlights but never before or since in a play called "Coitus Interruptus!"

With the same theme in mind, pianist Barney Bates, after experiencing the sudden movement of the Earth, descended to ground level as he and his partner fell through the first floor of an ageing warehouse, the Granary Jazz Club, in Bristol, when the unsafe floor gave way under his feet and their exertions.

Everyone with any knowledge of trombones realises how vulnerable the slide is. Roy Williams is, of course, no stranger to the care and attention required in their preservation. He failed on only two occasions! The first was a result of haste and ensuing panic. Arriving at Graeme Bayley's great club at Codsall one Saturday evening, probably slightly late, as was often the case, Roy put his trombone together and put it to his lips to warm up. He found something was obstructing the passage of air in the slide. In the absence of a 'pull through' he looked around for something to clear the obstruction. The only thing he could lay his hands on was a wire coat hanger. Realising the danger, he straightened it out and had a careful, experimental 'poke'. To his horror, the bloody thing disappeared down the slide and got stuck. What to do now? Poke another down there to remove the first. That got stuck too! But even worse the slide started to bulge! Disaster!

His second catastrophe was purely accidental. The band were performing at a ballroom in Boston, Lincolnshire. The audience were, shall we say, less than familiar with the fineries of jazz music, so Alex decided on our "All-dancing, sing-a-long" programme. The front of the stage was formed into a gentle curve, as I remember. In the middle of "Toot, Toot, Tootsie, Goodbye" which involved a sort of 'soft shoe shuffle' from the front line, Roy disappeared off the edge of the stage with a loud yell. The trombone flew in a trajectory and came to rest, slide down, on the parquet dance floor, ending up at a ninety-degree angle from the bell of the instrument. Fortunately, his good friend, Brian Casson, who, as a representative of the 'Besson Music Company' and who had supplied the instruments in question in the first place, came to his rescue on both occasions by simply being in attendance on the gigs and fortunately having a spare, his own, trombone in the boot of his car. Fortune favours the brave!

Certain places visited have their own special memories for me. While re-reading through this chapter, I am saddened to hear of a conflagration that has seen the end to the wonderful Stoke Severn Country Club, near Worcester. Owned by the fine cornet player and jazz aficionado, the late, John Richards and his wife, Gilly (who is still happily with us), the band was regularly welcomed by them, John's mother and a menagerie of pets and children, to perform a weekend of jazz 'n' booze. Hangovers were an unwelcome accompanist. John was later also an inspirational founder of the 'Upton Jazz Festival'. Although the edifice has 'gone up in smoke' memories of a fine establishment will live forever.

I have purposefully delayed mentioning two wonderful Jazz Clubs in the Southampton area for several reasons. The first must cover the friendly rivalry between the 'antagonistic' promoters of their clubs in their early years, situated less than twenty miles apart. I will describe them as I discovered them.

The first was in the suburbs of the city, itself. Run by a young enthusiast, sophisticated, moustachioed, Cole Mathieson, the 'Concorde' club, hosted in a function room of the "Bassett Arms" was one of the first I ever played in with the "Clydes". It was packed, hot and steamy and I seem to remember 'going down a bomb'. My visits there carried on into appearances with Alex's band always successfully performing to an enthusiastic and knowledgeable membership. But Cole was ambitious! Realising he could probably do much better if he purchased his own premises, he did just that. He bought a run-down, disused school house in nearby Eastleigh, converted it into a purpose-built club room with a stage and went from strength to strength. During the 1960s, Cole was a very important part of the success of the American visitors, presenting most or, indeed, all of them on their tours. Today, Cole is still actively promoting jazz at the 'Concorde' Club. Wisely extending his property to include residential rooms and a sophisticated dining area, Cole has succeeded in creating a country nightclub second to none. He has never deserted his roots, still featuring among the more modern, commercially successful musical trends, jazz of all styles twice-weekly.

His rival was an ex-Royal Navy seaman, greying, bearded, fourteen-pints-a-day, heavy smoking, wheezy, broad Hampshire-accented, enthusiast called Bob Champion. He ran his club in a pub called "The Dolphin", owned by a decorated ex-Spitfire pilot called Noel, in the rural village of Botley. As I described in the eulogy of my previous book, Bob's club was in every way just as important as Cole's. As time went by, Bob moved his sessions to the "Great Harry" pub in the beautiful yacht basin at Warsash.

We unfortunately lost Bob too early, but he is survived by his lovely wife, Andy and several children.

But the reason for delaying mentioning these wonderful clubs is because of one, revealing, hilarious escapade in "The Dolphin".

On setting off to the venue one afternoon, Lennie Hastings, proud owner of the "Lenvan", previously well-documented, said to me:

"You drive there and I'll drive back. That'll keep me off the booze!"

" I've heard that one before!",

I tendered.

"No! This time I'm serious!",

he replied.

So we drove off with yours truly at the wheel.

Of course he did! As a newt! Both of us! At the end of the evening, or probably early morning, we realised that neither of us could drive home. Noel graciously came to our rescue.

"You can have the guest room!",

he said.

"But it's a double bed!",

he continued, laughing to himself.

I couldn't have cared less if it was a perch in a hen-house, I was so pissed and tired. In bed, under the covers, back to back, wearing only shirts and underpants, the great drummer and a young guitarist, both drunk as skunks, tried to sleep.

Suddenly, I felt a strange sensation around my nether regions. Realising it was my bed mate's hand, I thought,

"Ah well!"

and reciprocated in a similar manner. I remember thinking:

"Well he is at least wearing make-up and has a wig, even if it is lying on the bedside table!"

We ended up, of course, in fits of laughter. Neither of us ever mentioned it again! I do remember it was me who drove home!

I am grateful to a couple of gentlemen who, on mentioning this memoir to them, very kindly reminded me of a few 'incidents' worth recalling:

We were booked to appear at the 'Great Yorkshire Jazz Festival' held in the Dales one summer in the 1970s. Typically, when we arrived, the wind was howling and the rain lashing down. The parking area was a sea of mud and stewards in sou'westers and wellies were trying to organize chaos. In the middle of the scene stood an instantly recognisable hearse, belonging to, of course, the redoubtable Diz

Disley.

"It's been called off! Abandoned! Multiple cases of hypothermia! They're bringing them up on stretchers – look, here's one now!"

Chuckling as he approached his vehicle his last words were:

"Typical Yorkshire bloody summer!"

My second tale also involves the great guitarist. I had been booked to appear for ten concerts with Stephane Grappelli, Diz and Len Skeat during a lean spell of work with the band. One of the concerts was in Farnham in Surrey and I had the dual honour of playing guitar and driving Steph and Diz back to London after the show. Just before we reached Virginia Water, I ran out petrol. Stephane was furious! In fact, I had never heard so many French-sounding,

English adjectives describing my dubious status before. Luckily, we were parked just at the opening to the drive of a mansion. Dutch courage guided my feet to the front door of the house and my hand to the doorbell. A pyjama-clad gentleman was just about to tear me off a strip when he heard the words "Stephane" and "Grappelli" emitting from my quivering lips.

"Do you think he would give me an autograph?",

he asked, at the same time donning an overcoat and pointing to a can of lawn mower petrol in a shed by the side of the house. Steph's attitude changed immediately, of course. His red countenance changed to a beaming smile and I was forgiven. *Ca ne fait rien, n'est pas?*

My final anecdote reveals a dubious record for the band. In Birmingham's Snow Hill area, a good jazz club, called "The Metro" had been established in one of the railway arches under the main line. We had built up a decent following there, a fact not unnoticed by the manager of the club. It was customary to be offered a nightcap after the performance. The night the record was broken for 'lateys,' as they were known, we surpassed ourselves. Nightcaps were substituted for their daytime equivalents as we sat at the bar. Suddenly there was a crash, as the band leader found himself on the floor. Not being the best sleeper in a bus, Alex was in the habit of occasionally taking a gentle sleeping pill to help the journey. This evening was no exception but, obviously, we were still at the bar when we should have been halfway home. It was the one and only time I ever saw Alex fall off a bar stool. The dubious record of being the latest-ever band to leave the club will stand forever, as the building is no longer there.

In mentioning our visits to America, Europe and Africa (although, in the former and the latter they consisted of only one area of each), I dealt with our unforgettable invitation to play at the Newport Jazz Festival in Rhode Island in my previous book. There is therefore no need to dwell on that, other than to emphasise what a wonderful experience it was for all of us. In Africa, we enjoyed the singular, similar visit to Saudi Arabia described a few paragraphs ago, but Europe offered a completely different picture for us.

My first departure from these Islands was, as you now know, to Germany in 1960, as I described in Chapter Three and I had to wait a few years before my next which, coincidentally, was to the same City of Mannheim and memorable for 'Beryl Bryden's Drawers'. The band had, before I joined, toured Switzerland for the Swiss equivalent of the Co-operative Society. Rene Hahn, their representative and a great fan of the band, re-invited us there. I remember Chris Staunton being on bass, trips on cablecars and John Barnes mucking about with an over-stuffed duvet (unknown in Britain at the time) on his bed after an imaginary 'substantial' meal.

We played concerts in France in Le Havre where we ate oysters, Paris with 'coq au vin', Antibes, where Bruce Turner (who was deputising for John) transported a bag of shredded vegetables all the way from home ("Can't be too careful, Dad!") and Nice, where I heard the devastating news of Lennie's death. On a lighter note, it was there we played with Wild Bill, Pee Wee Erwin, Johnnie Mince and Vic Dickenson and where, on the coach returning to our hotel, 'Sweets' Edison had an almighty rant about some colour-prejudiced incident he had experienced, oblivious to us in the back seat.

We visited Copenhagen and Odense in Denmark, where we avoided 'Elephant' ale in the capital and visited Hans Christian Anderson's house in the town of his birth. I also remember being disappointed at the size of the 'Little Mermaid' statue, expecting something on a much grander scale. It was at the club in Copenhagen, after our performance ended, that the promoter approached Alex with the words:

"Congratulations, Alex, you are the first band to all be on the stand at the end!"

He was, of course, referring to the effect 'Elephant' ale had on most bands, who seemed never to have achieved this. It was with a reference to the same brew that, when offered a bottle, I believe it was saxophonist, Al Cohn, who replied:

"No thanks Man! I drink to forget!"

(Norway took a while for me to get revenge on its Vikings, if "revenge" is the word when you are being invaded all over again by hospitality, but that is for another chronicle in a later book.) Sweden, on the other hand, offered an invitation to further jazz education in the University of Gothenburg. After an endless ferry crossing, we were dying for a beer. What we received was what they used to call 'near-beer'. In an effort to reduce problematic alcohol abuse, the Swedish Government had ordered a decrease in strength of its readily available alcohol. One sip brought Mickey Cooke's immortal riposte:

"It's like sex in a boat – Fucking near water!"

Although also attributed to Watney Brewery's infamous "Red Barrel" bitter, it was nevertheless hilarious at the time. Fortunately, one member of the band's discerning nose for the real thing, found a source where real Scotch whisky, gin and vodka, with the aid of a passport, could be purchased. The only remaining proviso required to fulfil the contract, was a bottomless purse.

The 'Fatherland', still divided by the 'Iron Curtain', provided our most frequent excursions abroad, at that time. Almost essentially being two countries, the diversity of their lifestyles was such that I will always remember them separately. The West, influenced by American and British 'progress', welcomed us with flashing lights, modern cars and fashionable clothes, but it still, with all its endeavour, couldn't shake off its Teutonic roots. In contrast, the Russian-influenced East was stark and had not visibly progressed much since the Iron Curtain had descended. There was one other notable difference – we mostly flew to the East and more frequently drove to the West, traversing Belgium and Holland, to arrive after several 'duty-free'- assisted hours at the cities on the Rhine, or in Bremen, Lubeck, Hamburg or wherever. They all had Jazz Clubs! "Doctor Jazz" Clubs in both Lubeck and Dusseldorf provided their own personal memories. On one occasion in the club in Lubeck, seated in the middle of the front row, a young lady sat knitting. The angle of her eyes matched that of her needles, with the result that I couldn't make up my mind whether she was watching me or Brian Lemon on the other side of the stage. Everything was revealed in the end. Approaching me as I was packing my guitar she said:

"I have a guitar at home. Will you come to my home and play it for me?"

On reaching her flat and opening the door, the first thing I noticed was that all the walls were covered in knitting. I sat down, accepted the drink she offered and the guitar she thrust in my hands.

"You are playing the 'Beatles'?", she asked.

I strummed 'Yesterday' or something similar. As I played, she started to disrobe, ending up completely 'starkers' and grinning from ear-to-ear. The rest of the evening is a blur, but I seem to remember one little fact – her eyes never straightened during the performance!

The band had a German friend called, believe it or not, Kris Kringel. Kris liked nothing better than to be 'one of the chaps.' On one occasion, rising late, wearing the mandatory 'iron turban,' we staggered to the *früstucksraum* just too late for breakfast. Asking the waiter if we could have a beer and perhaps a *wurst* and being told that that would be fine, we sat down at the table and waited…..and waited. Beers arrived and we waited…… Another beer came and still we waited………and waited. Suddenly, as the waiter came into sight, Herr Kringel leapt to his feet and loudly shouted in English:

"When do I become a sausage?"

The band's tours of the Deutsche Democratische Republik hold wonderful memories for me. Never was there a country of such contrasts. From our first stroll down the famous Unter den Linden in the historic part of bullet -strafed Berlin, at midnight on our arrival, with attendant Russian soldiers at various strategic points, to our first concert in Jena, famous for camera equipment, the country was a bewilderment to me. Cities and towns, unchanged for two decades imposed and yet, welcomed: Magdeburg, with its wonderful railway station; Zwickau where the soot from local coal mines immediately covered fresh snow falls; Karl Marx Stadt, formerly Chemnitz, with its hideous, huge bust of the communist idol; Erfurt where Martin Luther preached to his converts; the ruins after the destruction of Dresden; the glory that was the Weimar Republic, birth place of Goethe and site of Franz Liszt's house; Johann Sebastian Bach's organ in Leipzig: the Prussian palace of 'Sans Souci' and neighbouring Potsdam with all its historic inferences; the intrigue of Colditz Castle, now a 'Krankenhaus'; the despair of Buchenwald; the queues of people for a rare banana, while we gorged in the- restaurants of the 'Interhotels;

the knowledge and appreciation of the 'Classics' by the musically enlightened masses; the list goes on....

With Karl-Heinz Drechsel in Jena

Coming to the end of twenty-five years in jazz with its set patterns, its unexpected twists, its highs and lows and now, its uncertain future as far as mine was and is concerned, it would be remiss of me if I didn't, proudly, but without any sycophantic gloating, indulge in a little name-dropping. During my career, I rubbed shoulders with Benny Waters, Henry 'Red' Allen, Wild Bill Davison, Pee Wee Russell, Earl Hines, Bud Freeman, Peanuts Hucko, Eddie Miller, Ruby Braff, Rex Stewart, Willie the Lion Smith, Ben Webster, Eddie Lockjaw Davis, Billy Butterfield, Dick Wellstood, Joe Pass, Herb Ellis, Barney Kessel, Count Basie, Duke Ellington, his orchestra members, Stephane Grappelli, Lionel Hampton, Sam Woodyard, Nick Fatool, Bob Haggart, Yank Lawson, Dick Carey, Joe Venuti, Woody Herman, Bob Wilber, Kenny Davern and a handful more. When I started out and began to get interested in jazz, they were all merely heroic names to me.

Isn't life just wonderful? Although I must confess to be less than a believer in religion, especially orders and sects, mine so far has been blessed. For that alone I will be eternally grateful!

PART THREE

"Retirement"

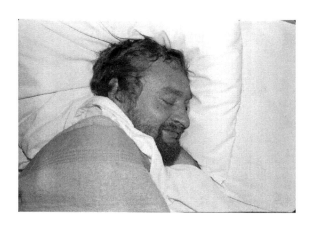

Chapter Twenty-three

"A Banana with a Moustache."

The envelope containing my Decree Absolute landed on the doormat with a loud thump. The sound came from my heart, of course, or was it perhaps the implosion of the last shreds of my dignity? It was certainly the "final nail in the coffin" containing my recently expired marriage. The half-expected news of my wife's affair had followed a series of excruciating sciatic back spasms during what was probably the worst Easter weekend in my thirty-eight-year existence.

The year was 1979. I was still a member of the Alex Welsh Band, which had recently endured a critical metamorphosis in personnel and style and which, together with the leader's declining health, had left me with serious decisions to make about my future. The musical direction of what, to me, was once a great outfit had been, in my view, put into reverse by Alex's decision to return to his Dixieland roots and, in the process, replace the two most iconic players in the band, at the whim of another, with others who, although great musicians in their own right, couldn't lace their jazz boots in my opinion. Should I head back north to my roots in Scotland or weather the storm and wait to see what happened? For a few months I dithered and swithered while the band personnel changed until the whole matter was resolved for me by another offer for the band to tour East Germany. This, I thought, would be a real opportunity to finally make up my mind. It certainly came close!

One of the side-effects I had endured throughout those eventful weeks during and immediately after my marriage break-up and divorce settlement, was a temporary psychological hatred and distrust of the 'fair' sex. I had tried blind dating and other ways, apart from the anathema of resorting to 'ladies of the night', to reassure myself of my masculinity. However, psychologically, I just couldn't bring myself to engage in any form of close relationship, not because I didn't fancy any of the ladies in question but because of a feeling of not being able to trust myself to successfully form such a personal friendship. It got so bad that I could hardly bear to touch a member of the opposite sex, even accidently, without feeling repulsion.

I welcomed the news that we were to re-visit the GDR for what turned out to be the band's final visit. Later, I was to travel there on two more occasions which I will tell you about as my tale unfolds in another volume. The musicians involved were: Alex, of course, Mickey Cooke, Al Gay, Fred Hunt, Roger Nobes, Ron Rubin and me. My first challenge presented itself on the very first night in Berlin, if I remember correctly. It could have been anywhere!   After the concert, we returned to the hotel and the night club. A bottle of bubbly seemed just the thing to get the tour off to a flyer. After finding a stool at the bar and opening a bottle, we were 'joined' by a few ladies. One of the chaps offered them a glass to which the answer was in the affirmative. Although their English was almost as poor as our German, we managed to strike up a sort of conversation. Inevitably things progressed and one of them suggested:

"Why not get another bottle and go to my place for a party?"

A couple of us thought this might be fun and a good chance to form a 'diplomatic' relationship. Safety in numbers, I thought and gaily went along with the idea. Of course you've guessed! As the bubbly and the party came to the end I found myself left with our hostess and her friend and partner. It was obvious what was expected. Well, of course I did! And what's more, I did every night for the next eighteen - with a different partner who employed virtually the same tactics. Every day I tried to sleep in the coach and failed miserably because of the hard suspension of the coach's under-carriage and the bumpy road surfaces left unrepaired from the war. So my 'ghost' was finally and emphatically laid to rest.

The tour, as usual, was a great musical success, although Alex was noticeably flagging by the end, as his health slowly deteriorated. It was memorable, apart from my shenanigans, for a couple of other regular occurrences. I had discovered J P Donleavy and was devouring his books while travelling. One of his fictional characters was named 'Rashers'. For one reason or another, this led to Ron's becoming 'Rashers' Rubin to which he retaliated by referring to me as 'Champagne Charlie.' We became very good friends and still are. He discovered a talent for composing Limerick poetry and had us in stitches with some he wrote about us. Later he successfully published a little book of his best efforts called "A Fanfare of Musical Limericks" which you should acquire at all costs. He will always be in my foreground of donators of everlasting musical statements. Among his finest were a couple of wonderful personal revelations and observations. He was a user of multi-vitamin capsules, which he purchased in little screw topped jars. When the contents had been duly consumed, they were replaced with Scotch whisky and re-labelled "Milk of Amnesia!" The second described the difference at the time, in the pub measures of his favourite beverage between its land of origin north of the border and its southern counterpart. This took the form of a term used in musical chording or intervals. Scotland was the land of the "augmented fifth" and England that of the "diminished sixth." Genius!

On my return from the GDR, the reality of my situation returned. A letter divulging the terms of my divorce informed me that I could keep everything in the house but not the house itself, which had to be shared. I had two choices: have the house valued and pay my ex-wife half of the value to remain there, or sell up and give her half of the profits after repaying the outstanding mortgage. I was 'graciously' allowed an undetermined time to consider, but eventually decided on the latter choice. Fred Hunt, our ex-piano player, came to my rescue. He had, some time after his return from an ill-advised move to South Africa, found a nice apartment in Byfleet, in Surrey, through registering with a Housing Association. By luck, the Association owned a block of flats in Luton and, with his help, I acquired one and moved in. From then on, my life took several different directions as I decided on my future.

By 1981, Alex was becoming more and more weakened and, although he had managed to stop drinking for a year or so, only succumbing to the 'demon' by having one glass of wine at Christmas, (one too many), had begun to realise that his body just couldn't take the rough and tumble lifestyle of the touring musician any longer. His wife, Maggie, was also having problems with alcohol and, in June 1982, she volunteered for self-detoxification by entering a rehabilitation centre. While she was there, Alex visited her and she noticed how desperately ill he looked. Later that day, worried sick, she asked her father and brothers to check on her husband's situation. After having no response on ringing the bell and knocking on the front door, they forcibly entered Alex's, home where they were shocked to find him in a distressing condition in bed. He was still resisting medical help when they had him moved to Hillingdon Hospital. On her last visit to his bedside, Maggie was told he had very little time left. Within a few days he was dead – exactly one week before his fifty third birthday.

During the last months of his debilitating illness, engagements had almost dried up. To make ends meet, I joined my friend, trombonist George Howden, in a morning job making bespoke sandwiches for a company called 'This 'n' That' in fashionable Shepherd Market in Mayfair.

Well, did we have some laughs!

George is a naturally funny fellow, anyway, but excelled himself in that job – much to the continual annoyance of the Scottish manageress, Mary. As we prepared the sandwiches, he would continually bombard me with material such as:

"I hurt myself when I was on holiday in Indonesia last month.

"Bangkok?",

I would ask.

"No, I grazed my elbow!",

he would reply.

"Oh shut up, George!",

Mary would yell across the floor from her position at the slicer.

We would have regular customers, of course: the incontinent old lady for her tub of egg mayonnaise - from whom everyone would run away, leaving me to serve; the young, handsome, slightly- balding builder, who sent one of our other ex-debutante helpers, Nicky, into gushing, drooling fits while serving him, and a middle-aged foreign gentleman whom Mary 'liked'. There was Gloria, the high-class hooker, who complained incessantly about her middle-eastern customers and well, you get the picture.

One day, the queue that usually formed outside the shop window was particularly long and, of course, as Murphy's Law would have it, everyone seemed to want to buy more than normal, slowing the whole process down. Just coming into view at the edge of the window, a new face appeared. He was obviously just fresh from public school, a fact later borne out by his 'posh' accent. As he approached the counter after a good twenty-minute delay, George told us to "leave this one" to him.

"What next?",

I thought.

Bearing in mind that there were trays of assorted filled rolls in the glass units on the counter, I must admit to being surprised at his request:

"I say, do you do cheese rolls?",

he uttered in flawless Oxford tones.

"Nah!   You   must   be   thinking   of   the sandwich shop just around the corner!",

replied George.

"Oh, thank you!",

replied the crestfallen fellow and he left the shop. Mary went berserk and ran out of the shop after him.

At the "Tally Ho", Kentish Town, publican Tom Horton and his Scottish wife Eileen, like us, enjoyed a "wee dram or twa'" which of course 'necessitated' the odd 'latey'. Musicians dropped in for a 'blow'. Among them were actor

Christopher Timothy, Barbara Dickson's drummer, Geoff and the young clarinettist Julian Stringle in the early years of what was to become a successful career. Great times but leading nowhere!

Next up was a stint with Pete Allen to help him out, while his father Bernie recuperated from a broken finger. Enjoyable as it was, with Mickey Cooke and Janus Carmello in the line-up, it wasn't the A W band.

Maybe I was looking for the impossible. The two most stabilising factors in my life had both crumbled. I did still see and play with Alex, but even that wasn't the band I had enjoyed so much! Please don't get me wrong! I was having a good time socially, spending my time between my flat in Luton and that of Mickey in the lovely Cotswold village of Stanford-in-the-Vale. Booze and women were, of course, a large part of it and I had a little money from the sale of my house.

I accepted Keith Smith's invitation to join his re-vamped 'Hefty Jazz' and, good as it was, with clarinettist, Ron Drake and Mickey Cooke, who had moved with me from Pete Allen, drummer Ron Hetherington, John Rodber on bass guitar and guest appearances by George Chisholm in the line-up, even with trips abroad, radio and television appearances at 'Pebble Mill' and a couple of recordings, it still wasn't anything like the A W band. What did I expect? What was I looking for? Did I really know?

Then a chance gig which presented a re-acquaintance with an old friend, turned the whole thing upside down!

Chapter Twenty-four

"Fives and Threes"

The brand new golf club on the Duke of Bedford's lovely estate, Woburn, famous, of course, for the Abbey, the nearby Georgian village and more recently opened "Safari Park," was entertaining visitors to its most up-market tournament so far, the "Dunlop British Masters." I decided I deserved a day out and a golf lesson to boot and was strolling from the car park in the direction of where the 'action' was, when I received a tap on my shoulder.

"Jim, it is you! What are you doing in this neck of the woods?",

a Northern-accented voice inquired.

"I could ask you the same question",

I replied. I hadn't seen Bill Holleran for years – from the time of Alex's successful concerts at the Manchester Sports Guild and the Bolton Yacht Club, in fact.

"Well, I ran a little painting and decorating business involved with the developing Milton Keynes estates and I had a place in Woburn, but the missus and I split up and I moved into a little cottage not far from here. But I spend most of my time in the Wine

Lodge in the village now, doing a little bit of this and that. Are you living locally?"

I filled him in on my recent unfortunate developments, finishing off by describing my flat in Luton and my indecision over my future.

"Ee, we can't have you giving it up! Would you be interested in doing a spot with a local band, the "Wayfarers" in The "Magpie" pub tomorrow night? I'm running it with Mac McLaren, who used to run jazz nights in Brighton. He'd be delighted and so would the band."

I accepted his invitation and agreed to meet him at the Wine Lodge next evening for some "home-made meat 'n' potato pie and a pint" before the gig. As usual, I arrived too early the next afternoon and, with nothing much to do, thought I'd do a little window-shopping and exploration of the beautiful Georgian village. I had hardly parked my car when an attractive, middle-aged lady came running after me, calling

"Jim, are you Jim Douglas?"

I answered in the affirmative and was immediately whisked into a bay-windowed café/bar and told to take a seat and asked:

"What would you like to drink? Welcome to the Wine Lodge!"

Jill Christian owned and managed the establishment which, together with the 'Magpie' Hotel, was to dominate my leisure hours for the next year or so. Jill, a divorcee, was the daughter of an ex-champion jockey and had three children, the eldest, Simon, a race horse trainer, Louise, known familiarly as 'Lulu', her middle child, who worked in the lodge and a younger son, Giles. It became clear to me very quickly that this was one of the focal points for visitors to the village and the more middle-class residents who preferred a glass of wine to a pint of beer, which was readily available at the other licensed establishments.

I was, as I have implied, welcomed with open arms and soon got to know the regular customers. I got involved in domino matches, playing the 'fives and threes' rules and was often encouraged to accompany after-hours sing songs. I also became an integral part of regular jazz sessions at the 'Magpie', organised by landlord 'Mac' McLaren, who had, in a previous tenancy, run jazz in Brighton and who, while there, had befriended the great trumpeter, Kenny Baker and superb tenor player, Danny Moss, who both came to gigs at the pub. Danny brought his lovely wife and great singer, Jeannie Lamb, on most of his engagements and we were also delighted by impromptu visits by the wonderful trombonist George Chisholm, who had taken up residence locally.

I took to spending more and more of my spare time in Woburn and less and less at my Luton base, although I did entertain some friends, mostly of the opposite sex, there, including one or two from the village, who were pleased to spend some time away from gossiping neighbours. I had also made acquaintance with a lady from the Birmingham area, another from Newbury, who broke a holiday arrangement in Greece, using me as her excuse, and one who travelled all the way from Lancaster for the occasional weekend, but none of them was in a mood to form a permanent relationship and nor indeed was I. Although still officially a member of Alex's band, I was playing most of the time with Keith Smith, Pete Allen and, occasionally, Dave Shepherd.

The remainder of my spare time I spent with friends in London. Doug Bence, a journalist for the Daily Mirror and his partner, Duffy, rented a flat near Chalk Farm. We had met by chance, found we had lots in common and began spending Sunday lunchtimes in different watering holes, ending up at his flat where I could 'put my head down' for an hour or two before resuming our Bacchanalian adventure. Doug played guitar too, so we had lots of great impromptu sessions. We still keep in touch, although he has retired to the West country.

It was during this transitional period that I made the first of several career and life-changing mistakes. In all the years I had been playing, I had always only been answerable to one band leader at a time. Suddenly, I was being offered gigs from many sources and I didn't know how to say "no", with the result, of course, that I found myself "double-booked" on several occasions. Not to mince words, I let too many people down.

Firstly, it was Alex who, on a trip to Jersey, was, to his surprise, suddenly confronted with Paul Sealey's arrival at the Portsmouth

Docks in my place. Then, on the way to a gig in Salisbury for Pete Allen, which I wasn't looking forward to, I got as far as Newbury and drove all the way around a roundabout and headed home. Worse was to follow, although, to this day, I don't accept full responsibility for my decision not to, at the very last minute, travel to East Germany with Dave Shepherd. I had informed Keith Smith of my engagement, asking to be excused one gig, an appearance at a concert in Bath. On the morning of the flight I was informed by Keith that I had been billed to appear and, as there was no pianist, he was depending on me. Ignoring all Dave's attempts to reach me by telephone, I failed to appear at the airport and hurried down to Bath, where the first person I met was pianist Ralph Laing, who was, of course, booked on the gig. I was furious with Keith who, in a somewhat annoying manner, just laughed it off. I don't think Dave ever forgave me for that and rightly so!

Cowardly behaviour, you might think, and you are, of course, right. I could quite easily have sorted something out by answering or picking up the phone. Perhaps so, but I didn't. This "cowardice" happened several times over the next decade or so and I am afraid I let down several colleagues, such as Pete, Alan Elsdon and Bob Bates in the process. I became "Mr Unreliable." To this day I am deeply sorry for my actions and consider myself lucky that I was ever re-booked by anyone. It won't happen again!

So, having 'pissed off' quite a few old friends and new, I was lucky to still have somewhere to play. With the exception of gigs with local musicians and the occasional one with drummer, Bob Guthrie, in North London, my living came mainly from the direction of Keith Smith's 'Hefty Jazz'. To be fair, there was plenty of talent in its ranks and gigs were becoming plentiful, varying from sessions in jazz clubs to radio at Pebble Mill and the occasional TV spot I have already mentioned. There were concerts too, with special guest, George Chisholm, for this fine band, which featured Mickey Cooke and Ron

Drake and a long playing album, "Salute to Satchmo" was cut and issued. We went to France, where the band leader was billed as "Keez Schmidt" and where I had frog's legs for dinner for the first time. A concert at the Dresden Dixieland Festival, in or around 1980, was filmed and can now be viewed on "YouTube".

During the latter years of my marriage, I had gradually built up an enjoyment of cooking, especially for dinner parties, which we hosted regularly. I became more and more adventurous with my menus and started collecting weekly publications of "Carrier's Kitchen", which I devoured eagerly. (Please excuse the pun!)

So, by the time I was splitting my residential time between Luton, London and Woburn, I had become quite proficient in the culinary sciences. I had befriended a City Banker named Tom Quinn, whom I met in our many domino matches. He owned number six, Bedford Street, a lovely bay-windowed

Georgian, terraced house, once the residence of Hugh Gaitskell, the Labour Leader. Next door, a co-joined, partly fifteenth century house made up of numbers four and five, was used as a costume and fancy dress shop. The owner decided to downsize her business and move away from the village. She put the property on the market. Tom decided to make an offer and was successful. For the next eighteen months or thereabouts, the circle of his life and that of my own, took on another tangent.

Chapter Twenty-five

"Sixes and Sevens"

One Saturday evening, I had arranged a party at my Luton flat, to which I had invited most of my domino-playing friends. Bill was there, as was a current girlfriend, Ruth. There were about twenty in all and, right at the forefront, with all of his larger than life persona, were Tom Quinn and his partner Sue, who was a member of the backroom staff at the Wine Lodge. Wine, beer and whisky flowed, of course. I had spent a couple of days preparing a buffet supper and was pleased with the resulting 'banquet' I presented to my guests. At some stage, Tom came to me to ask who my caterer was and, on my reply, said:

"You and I need to have a serious talk! One o'clock tomorrow in the Lodge - O.K.?"

I answered that that would be fine, saying I had intended to go there anyway. A short time later I retired to bed, a little drunk, but curious about what Mr. Quinn had in mind.

The next day I entered the Wine Lodge at about twelve thirty to find a game of dominoes already underway and a place reserved for me at the table.

"The usual?" ,

asked Tom.

"Yes, please!",

I replied, as I took my seat.

The game continued and my curiosity as to what Tom wanted to discuss with me almost took over. At last, match over, we repaired to the bar.

"Where did you learn to cook like that?"

were almost his first words. Replying that I was entirely self-taught, although I did have a younger brother, who was a chef and that it was just a hobby, he went on:

"Thought about doing it for a living?"

I replied I had never considered it but, as I was not sure in which direction my future lay....

"Let me put you in the picture!",

he interrupted.

"As you know, I have bought the house next door as a future investment, but wasn't sure what to do with it. You know it's a fifteenth century listed building, don't you? Well! Last night you came up with what I think might be the answer to both our problems. How do you fancy being the chef of a French restaurant? Simple French country food, cooked nicely and presented in the perfect environment?"

"I'm not sure I have enough experience to

cook to order in a full restaurant, and ...."

I was interrupted again...

"There will only be twenty-four seats and the menu very small and consisting mostly of pre-cooked dishes like *Cassoulet* .... but no frozen stuff..."

He had it all worked out in his mind!

"You and Sue can go off on a course, while alterations are in progress. Robert Carrier is advertising on television some courses at his place in Suffolk. *Nouvelle Cuisine,* mind you, but good experience..."

on and on he went. All the time, a little bubble

of excitement was forming in the pit of my stomach.

"When it's ready, or before, for that matter, you could move into the house and even sell your flat!" ...

his brain was in overdrive! I thanked him for his offer and his faith in me and told him I would sleep on it. This was another falsehood on my part as the next two nights were pretty sleepless. I tossed and turned and juggled with the pros and cons, which always seem a thousand times manifold in the middle of the night.

I had enough gigs to keep me going, mostly in the Cotswold area with Keith, who had taken up residence in Burford, especially in the local hostelries, where he had introduced me to the great Welsh actor, Freddie Jones. I was, however, getting more and more travel-weary in the process. A tour of "Salute to Satchmo" to

Scotland and the North West hammered the last nail in the coffin. I drove hundreds of miles on my own, ending up late for a concert in Southport, with a journey back to Luton facing me afterwards.

My mind was made up! I informed Tom I would be delighted to take him at his word and offered to get down to business right away. I told Keith, who insisted I fulfil the gigs I had agreed and I gradually cut down on playing.

For the next few weeks, I carried on as usual, with one or two notable exceptions to do with cooking, of course. I spent time in the kitchen at Woburn, learning the basic sauces and techniques I would require in my new career. Sue and I went on the Carrier course, staying the two weeks in a little guest house nearby.

I had no idea how much I didn't know! But I was willing to learn and threw myself into the lectures with gusto. At the end of the two weeks I was presented with two certificates of achievement, which hang on my dining room wall to this day and was interviewed by Anglia Television for a magazine programme about cooking.

The next step was to plan the restaurant and kitchen.

All the time this was going on, I was still playing enough gigs to keep the wolf from the door. Drummer, Laurie Chescoe, who was also involved with a DIY company, offered me promotional engagements on a bus top or back of a lorry playing banjo with "Fads Army!" I continued my visits to Oxfordshire for Keith and played, as usual, with the local band the "Wayfarers" at the "Magpie" and other pubs in the vicinity. I also appeared on what were to be Alex's final two engagements in Nottingham and at the "100 Club" in Oxford Street. The news brought to me by telephone in my Luton home a few weeks later that Alex had been hospitalised and was seriously ill came as no surprise, but was still a shock to me. I was doubly surprised to hear that Maggie had volunteered herself to undertake a detoxification programme and was not at home when he was discovered very ill by her family. She had been desperately worried about his welfare and had asked her father and brother to check on him. He died just over a week later. His funeral and wake was attended by almost everyone in the jazz fraternity. Trombonist Mickey Cooke, well-known for his dry sense of humour, observed that he would "Probably be late for his own funeral!" and he was a little. The party, at the West London Hotel, the "Master Robert" was even better attended and his memorable life well toasted and remembered in anecdotes. As I was leaving, I asked Maggie if there was anything I could do to help her through this trying time and to give me a ring if she needed anything. A week or so later she called me and left a message to say she was back home with her parents. I called her back the same day and after asking if I could help, she replied "You could take me out to dinner!" I knew exactly what she meant. She needed a break from all the pressures of the last few harrowing months she had endured and saw in me a friend whom she could maybe just relax with and talk to. We didn't dine out, but I invited her to accompany me on a few gigs with Bob Guthrie's band in the Finchley area of North London. After packing my car at the end of one gig and before she drove off back to Greenford, where she lived, I asked her to join me in the front of my car to ask her if she had enjoyed herself and whether she would like to go out again. She replied that she would love to. I leant toward her to give her a little goodnight kiss. This is not a revelation of our love life, so don't raise your hopes! One little kiss led to another and then a longer one......enough! Nice kisses, I thought! She got into her car and we went our separate ways home.

Maggie had come on the scene at Steve Duman's jazz club at the "Whittington" at Pinner in February 1969, as I explained in a previous chapter. It's worth repeating that, with her Titian red bobbed hair, infectious wide grin and her slim figure clad in a black 'mini' dress cut high enough to show off her well-proportioned legs, she was stunning! I found out later that she had formed a high opinion of the music she heard that evening. She had no prior knowledge of the band and told me she had expected a sort of slightly inferior Acker Bilk. Totally swept away with the versatility of the musicians and especially by a solo by Roy Williams of a favourite of hers, "Here's that Rainy Day", she revealed to me that she had gone home to her music-loving parents and enthused over the evening, telling her father:

"Oh Dad, what a lovely band I heard tonight!"

After several "push-me-pull-you" years of separations and reparations, Alex and Maggie were married in 1977.

As I have hinted, a lot of water flowed under the bridge between that fateful first evening and Alex's untimely death in 1982. As a dedicated rower on that river, I will from time to time, "lean on my oar" and recall my side of it. Suffice to say for now that my marriage vows of less than two years had been slightly ruffled at the Whittington and sorely tried in the August of the same year, when the four of us shared our holiday in Majorca.

But, back to 1982. The next few weeks are a little cloudy in my memory, but I do know we met again a couple of times and she even helped some of us by sorting out travel arrangements for a trip to Zurich's "Limatt 44" jazz club with Keith. I asked her if she would like to look after my car, a nice white 2L S Cortina, while we were gone. She replied she would be delighted to do so. During this break away from each other, I started to wonder if things between us were maybe moving a little too fast. Though these feelings were irrational and perhaps unwelcome, they nevertheless entered my thoughts. After all, we had both endured traumatic break-ups with our previous partners and the thought of hurting her more or, for that matter, being hurt myself, started to weigh heavily on my mind in the solitude of my hotel room. I wrote her an ill-conceived letter, trying and (I found out at a later date) failing abjectly, to convey my thoughts on paper. It must have come as quite a disappointment to her to read my unemotional words which even covered her leaving the car and keys somewhere. Fortunately, I thought about it again and realising how much I wanted to see her, rearranged to meet her. I had just made the best decision of my entire life.

The initial work on the restaurant was complete and I spent more and more time in the empty fifteenth century, seven or eight-bedroom property which consisted of numbers five and six Bedford Street. I kept my flat which, of course, still contained most of my belongings, but hardly set foot in it. There was sufficient furniture in the rest of the house above the restaurant to make it habitable but, as Maggie and I were spending more and more time together there, it became obvious that it would suit all purposes if I removed my belongings and furniture there and put my flat, which I had bought outright, on the property market. Maggie had already negotiated the sale of her property in Ruislip and being ready to settle into a new life with me, helped me to set up our home in Woburn. The flat sold quickly and the ties to our former lives ended.

To say the next twelve months or so were adventurous would be to grossly underestimate our new lifestyle. The end result was our marriage and the birth of our son, Will. But that would fill another book! Perhaps I'll attempt a 'trilogy'! There has been plenty of 'travelitis' since then, perhaps enough to to fill maybe two!

The End

Printed in Great Britain
· by Amazon